'I know thousands of Christian_____
like this. For decades we have _____
and community redemption, a _____
Gary and Hannah and their te_____
made it work. I respect them n_____
an eyewitness on many occasi_____
community benefited from all t_____ ...y are truly carrying the
anointing of the early Salvationists!'

Debra Green, Director of City Links

'Gary Bishop writes with a warmth and fluency that draws the
reader in from the very first word. And he tells stories in a way
that makes each character and each scene come to life. But this is
not a "good read" in the way we usually mean that phrase. If you
want to settle down by the fire with a cup of coffee and enjoy an
evening's escapism, this is definitely not the book for you! For Gary
tells true stories, harrowing stories from "Darkest England" in the
twenty-first century, stories that he has witnessed at first hand and
in which he has usually played a significant role.

'The result is a little book with a massive challenge. Taking his
title and his inspiration from William Booth's *In Darkest England
and the Way Out*, Gary is brave enough to go even further than
his literary mentor. It's no longer enough for the church to make
the occasional foray into the inner city, rescue a few individuals
and then move out again. The real challenge is for individuals and
groups to relocate from comfortable suburbia, to settle in "Darkest
England", and to create loving, accepting communities where they
don't and won't otherwise exist. Gary, his wife Hannah, and the
other members of the Eden Openshaw team have done just that
for the last seven years. The question this book forces us to face is
this: "Who is willing to follow their example?"'

Chick Yuill

'I cannot share Gary Bishop's faith but I have nothing but admiration for the work he and his team have done in East Manchester. Many of us take pride in our social consciences but our compassion commutes: we live not where we care. But Gary has moved into an area of great need and in this passionate book shows us what faith in action means today. It is a moving testimony, an account of a wish to work with local people and so bring light to the dark zones beyond the central glitz of one of Britain's biggest cities.'

David Ward, *The Guardian*

'I'd like to be more like Gary when I grow up! While keeping it real, Gary's engaging style provides a hopeful manifesto for any church or Christian trying to make a difference downtown.'

Russell Rook, Chief Executive of Chapel St and chair of the Spring Harvest Theme Team

DARKEST ENGLAND & THE WAY BACK IN

GARY BISHOP

Authentic

MILTON KEYNES ● COLORADO SPRINGS ● HYDERABAD

THANKS

A book like this is never the work of just one person; the stories told and lessons learned are the fruit of a collective journey that I have shared with so many friends. It has been my privilege to write it all down. I am especially grateful to all our family at Openshaw Community Church who live the Darkest England experience with us and who have taught us so much about life, community, love and ultimately about God.

Big thanks to Russ for being a constant friend and for encouraging me to write this book; to Chick and Margaret for being the most amazing mentors, bosses and friends – you set us free to be the people we have needed to be. To Sam and Nic for helping us to carry the vision and the burden and now for taking it to the next level.

To Dev who edited and Lloyd who designed this book – you guys have gone way beyond the call of duty to make it all happen and I am really grateful to you. I'm also grateful to Katy who believed in my idea for the cover and took a picture which, for me, summarises the book perfectly.

Many people appear in the pages of this book. I have spoken to lots of you and I'm grateful that you've allowed me to use your stories. Most of the names have been changed but those people who have been close to the stories which I tell will easily recognise themselves and others.

If you find yourself in these pages I trust that you will find the accounts both truthful and respectful. Most importantly I am grateful for the way in which you have each blessed, encouraged, challenged, shaped and taught us.

Special thanks to David Westlake, Esther Stansfield and Tim Chester who have given me permission to extensively quote their work, especially in chapter 2, and to Tommy who contributed so generously to chapter 5.

This book owes a huge debt to our great friend Gretta. What a legend you are! This really, really would never have happened without you. Your encouragement, your research, your critical reading, your red pen and your enthusiasm for the book have kept the whole project moving and on track. You have given so much without return, thank you doesn't seem enough.

To our mums, dads and families, we know that in lots of ways you make the greatest sacrifice by being absent from 'the kids' for months at a time but you support us regardless and that means the world to us.

Finally, huge love and thanks to Hannah. It is your passion that took us to Darkest England in the first place – this is your story as much as it is mine. To Joel and Jeya who inspire us every day to dream of the best for the children of our neighbourhood.

Praise the Lord O my Soul; all my inmost being,
praise his holy name

CONTENTS

FOREWORD
ANDY HAWTHORNE

Doing what I do, I get to read a lot of Christian books. I have even been asked to write the foreword to quite a few. I can't remember, however, for a long, long time one that moved me quite as much as the one you have in your hand.

As I put it down and read the last remarkable quote from the legendary General Booth, the thought that went through my mind was that surely much of the church in the UK has lost the plot. How much have our endless rounds of meetings and our 'under-the-bowl' pampering for the 'in crowd' got to do with following our Jesus who 'didn't come to reach the healthy but the sick'?

Gary's book isn't some pious theological tome that speaks of God's heart for the poor but doesn't give us any clue as to how to get involved in the grit and grime of their messy lives. This is real, authentic, twenty-first-century Jesus following. In the Gospels, much of Jesus' ministry is described through a series of encounters with messed-up humanity – individual after individual cuts across the Master's plans, bringing all their baggage and hang-ups with them, and then goes away transformed.

I've watched Gary's ministry over the last seven years in Openshaw and whilst sadly he isn't regularly seeing the dead raised and legions of demons fleeing, I honestly can't think of anything going on in this country that follows Jesus' model closer.

So read on and get ready to be challenged to the core of your being – and please whatever you do, don't put the book down without seriously asking yourself, 'What am I doing and what am I prepared to sacrifice to reach the poor and the needy in Darkest England and beyond in my generation?'

Andy Hawthorne, Director, The Message Trust

In 1891 General William Booth, founder of the Salvation Army, published his best-known work, *In Darkest England and The Way Out*. His book outlined a plan which he believed would rescue the masses of people living in the slums of Great Britain and propel them to better lives in the country and overseas through a series of programmes and colonies. It was Booth's belief that every human being should have the opportunity to experience a two-dimensional salvation which consists of spiritual regeneration through faith in Jesus Christ and also 'social salvation', by which he meant relief from the wretched grip of poverty, worklessness, addiction and crime.[1] Booth's book had an immediate and far-reaching impact on Victorian Britain and subsequently throughout the world. He sold 200,000 copies within the first year, and within nine years of its first publication, The Salvation Army had served 27 million cheap meals, lodged 11 million homeless people, traced 18,000 missing people and found jobs for 9,000 unemployed people. Booth's book was used as a blueprint for the present-day welfare state when it was set up by the government in 1948, and many of Booth's ideas were incorporated into the welfare state system.

Having read *In Darkest England and The Way Out* I was inspired to write this book, not to contradict Booth's masterpiece, but in the hope that my experiences in twenty-first-century Darkest England might shed some fresh light on his timeless vision for reaching out into the margins of our broken society. If this book does nothing more than inspire us to read Booth's book again and sense once more his passion for the poor, lost men and women of the underclasses then it will have achieved a good thing. My hope is that it does something more than that. I hope that from the pages of this book you will hear a siren call from the streets of our most deprived communities which begs our churches to take their responsibility for the poor seriously, and pleads with you to slip off your polished shoes and take a walk into a world which is anxiously waiting for the salvation light which you carry.

Salvation Army history is littered with captivating stories of how Salvationists have worked for both the eternal and temporal salvation of mankind. One of my favourite stories is that of the early missionaries to India, Major Booth-Tucker and Arnold Weerasooriva[2] who, clad in the traditional dress of Indian holy men, wandered from village to village to preach the Gospel. Sometimes they were welcomed and sometimes rejected, but one particular village refused them even a cup of water. Exhausted from the searing heat and disappointed at the hostility with which they had been met, the two men took shelter under a tamarind tree a little way outside the village, where they both fell asleep. As they slept, some of the curious villagers gathered around the two sleeping men and noticed that the soles of their bare feet were covered in sores and blisters from walking on the hot, unforgiving paths without shoes. The villagers were so struck by the sacrifice of these men that they sat at a distance and watched them sleep. When Booth-Tucker awoke and realised he had a congregation he took out his Bible and began to read. The villagers asked questions and soon the two companions were invited into the village, offered hospitality, and asked to share the Gospel with all the natives. Fredrick Booth-Tucker later remarked, 'I preached my best sermon with my feet.'

There is a vulnerability about walking somewhere without shoes. You know that you are going to have to walk carefully because the soles of our feet are very sensitive and bruise easily, and jagged flints and broken glass will easily pierce the skin. You can be sure that even if no serious injuries occur, the muck and grime of the place you are walking will quickly adhere itself to your skin and most likely be difficult to remove. These are the thoughts behind the cover of this book; the journey back into Darkest England must be one of strength and courage but at the same time it must be one of weakness and vulnerability. There is no doubt that the journey will be costly and painful as well as fulfilling and exciting. We will need to be people who are secure enough in our personal and spiritual identity that we are prepared to be moulded and affected by the culture into which we migrate, accepting its peculiarities and calling it home.

The title given to this book does not limit its usefulness to the shores of England or indeed to the UK. Many of the principles I explore here will be transferable to contexts across the world. I gave some considerable thought to changing the name of the book in order to avoid causing any offence, but this title worked so well that I decided to stick with it in the hope that readers would understand the heart behind it rather than feel excluded. I hope this is so.

THE OPENSHAW EDEN PROJECT

In May 2000, The Salvation Army and The Message Trust launched an initiative in Openshaw, an inner-city housing estate in East Manchester. The initiative followed a model called EDEN, which had previously been started in Wythenshawe and Langworthy (Salford). The vision for these (and the other seven projects that have started since) is to move large groups of Christians into the toughest and poorest estates around the city to work primarily with young people, ensuring that they have opportunities to hear and understand the Gospel and to provide environments where Christian faith can thrive and grow within youth culture.

Between May and November 2000, 16 young Christians moved into one of the most troubled areas of the Openshaw estate. With four full-time employees and a growing group of volunteer youth workers, the team began to initiate outreach and detached youth work on the streets. With the support and backing of The Salvation Army and The Message, the team also began to meet together for worship on Sundays in the old, disused 'Army' hall which stands in a central location in the community. At that time there was no template or model given to the church, other than to live out the Gospel and create a church that local people could access. Many of our experiences are recorded in the chapters of this book – many joys, many sorrows and many lessons learned. There are lots of ways in which the principles outlined might be achieved in other contexts but I want to share some of the amazing Eden story and draw some lessons from it which may be of use as we, the church of Jesus Christ, seek to discover our destiny in the twenty-first century.

References and Notes

1. Booth, W., *In Darkest England and the Way Out* (IndyPress.com), p. 30.
2. This well-known Salvation Army story is found in Williams, H. Booth-Tucker, *William Booth's First Gentleman* (Hodder & Stoughton, 1980), and Unsworth, M., *Bridging the Gap* (Eagle Books), No 52. With thanks to the Salvation Army International Heritage Centre for their help in tracing this story.

.1

WELCOME TO TWENTY-FIRST-CENTURY DARKEST ENGLAND

Early one winter evening I made my way to visit a man and his two teenaged sons. Education Welfare had contacted us at the Eden Project to ask if we could provide any support for this family. First calls are always unnerving, and this one was no different. It was obvious at first sight that this dwelling was little more than a squat, with the windows boarded and the door so splintered around the lock that it no longer held shut on its own – a sure sign that this house had been raided by police, and no doubt others, on more than one occasion. I pushed the door, knocked and shouted all at the same time, mostly for my own benefit. I heard the clanking of cutlery and a tall, lanky man strode into the dark hallway. 'Hiya,' he bellowed in a thick Mancunian accent and greeted me with a warm, vice-like handshake. I introduced myself saying I was from the church and he invited me in, introducing himself as Tony.

The stench in the house was pungent. I could see down the hallway and through the kitchen: brown moth-eaten rags hanging at a smashed window pretending to be curtains, and a kitchen sink black with dirt and grease. My boots clunked on the bare floorboards as I followed Tony into the lounge. There I met Justin and David (aged 11 and 13) for the first time, two of the loveliest boys I have ever met, dressed in what could just about pass for school uniform. The television provided the only light in the room, and as we talked over its noise all their faces were lit up in glorious technicolour. They each had a huge plate of mashed potato covered in gravy, a rare feast prepared by a loving Dad for his children. No explanation or excuse was offered for the drug paraphernalia which lay openly on display on a box in the middle of the room: a lighter, a packet of Rizla skins, charred foil and some old tobacco tins. They did not draw attention to them and neither did I.

The story that unfolded, and continues to unfold, is worth a book in itself but part of the tragedy is that for five months this little family had been in debt to a loan shark. What started as a £40 advance to feed Tony's habit had got them trapped in the grip of a merciless oppressor who confiscated Tony's benefit book, accompanied him every week to the post office and took all of the £107 which he received to keep him and his boys alive. The randomly calculated interest on the loan meant that the debt always outweighed the ability to pay. The threat of violence and of harm coming to the boys prevented any cry for help, so all that Tony and the boys could do was scavenge for out-of-date food in the skip at the back of Kwik Save, beg and steal what they could to survive and pray to God that somehow things would change, somehow things would get better. Now here I was, being welcomed into this paradoxical world of love and fear, laughter and tears, hope and despair – being welcomed into Darkest England.

Living in Openshaw means that even a quiet afternoon walk can be a revelation. I approached three boys in the park late one summer afternoon, recognising them all from our kids' club. As I got closer they noticed me and scuffled around in a futile attempt to conceal something from my view. The two-litre bottle of WKD alcopop was too large to be hidden in the clothing that the three 8- and 9-year-olds were wearing, and the boys quickly conceded defeat and slightly nervously showed me the half-empty container. When I asked them why they were drinking, they told me that England had lost their football match today so they were drowning their sorrows – this made perfect sense to them. After a short conversation the boys wisely concluded that they would rather pour the drink away than have me divulge their secret to their mums, and I carried on my walk wondering how such perverse logic can find its way into the mind of ones so young.

On the next corner I found my answer. Outside our local pub were crowds of men: fathers, grandfathers, role models to our children, 'drowning their sorrows'. The irony is that this scene would have been identical had England won their football match, but the justification would have been celebration rather than sorrow. And this is much of the story of Darkest England – alcohol accompanies every occasion, a birth, a death, an anniversary, a christening.

Perhaps the strangest drink-fuelled celebration I heard of was the day when George Best died. The great Manchester United legend, whose very public battle with alcoholism eventually cost him his life, was commemorated in the most inappropriate fashion. Alcohol has become a god to many in these communities, it's the thing that life is organised around, the thing that orders the calendar and marks every occasion, that empties the wallets of the old and bellies of the young. I was recently interviewed on a radio show about youth binge drinking, a regular media favourite, and asked, 'Why do you think young people binge drink?' The only answer I could think to give was 'Children copy adults.'

These are not isolated incidents; it is by no means unusual to discover a family in our community with literally no food and no money for the gas meter. It's easy to find children who play, unaccompanied, on the streets until midnight and beyond wearing their school uniforms because that is the only clothing they have, or parents who are too busy or too preoccupied to care about the needs of their kids or just too poor to make meagre funds stretch from one week's end to the other. I hear the cries from the suburban semis and the comfy church pews: 'How is this possible? Surely not in twenty-first-century England, with all its affluent civilisation and the generosity of the welfare system?' It happens because a working mother whose husband refuses to work cannot feed her three children and keep her house afloat on the minimum wage. It happens because if your mum has a heroin or alcohol addiction her first priority on benefit day will not be the weekly shop at Asda. It happens often because one member of a family makes poor choices which lock the others into a desperate cycle of poverty.

STRANGERS AND ALIENS

You do not have to live in Darkest England for long before you realise who you are and where you come from. Within a few short weeks of living in the inner city I became acutely aware that I have had an immensely privileged upbringing, something that, to my shame, had never occurred to me before. Like most of us I have always presumed that my experience of life is the benchmark for normality. My childhood memories of a loving family with hard-working parents, holidays, comfortable houses, clean clothes and the mouth-watering aroma of a wide variety of Mum's cooking filling the house every evening are nothing more than an unimaginable dream to the native children of my new community. Worse than that: as a child of this community your personal safety cannot be guaranteed, as the levels of violence behind the closed doors of private homes and in public spaces means that inevitably innocent bystanders get caught in the crossfire. At a kids' club New Year party we asked a child, 'Did you enjoy Christmas?' Her response was a poignant reminder of just how unfamiliar this land is to me – 'My mum's boyfriend smashed a mirror over her head so we spent most of it in hospital.' A far cry from the cosy, indulgent celebrations of my childhood with open fires and dusty LPs sounding out their sentimental festive tunes.

Having grown up in a commuter belt on the south coast, many of my neighbours had been businessmen and women who travelled to London daily for their work, high flyers who left home early in pinstriped suits with briefcases and umbrellas and returned home late in as pristine a condition as when they left: lawyers, bankers, teachers, and then a few families like mine who had made enough money through running a small business to climb the dizzy heights of suburbia. This is of course a generalisation, because in the suburbs you don't ever really get to know what goes on next door. The distance between your front door and the one opposite is a good 40 metres, and that through the thick foliage of the front garden, the secure fortress of iron fencing and the shingle drive which, if it were legal, would surely be replaced by a moat with a drawbridge. There is no doubt that such communities hold their own brand of darkness, with wives still beaten, husbands mistreated, and children abused, and loneliness and misery are present here too. However, the difference in Darkest England is that poverty creates lives so full of struggle that if you manage to resist turning to alcohol to anaesthetise the boredom, and manage to prevent yourself from hitting out at your husband or wife in frustration that you cannot earn enough money to pay the bills, then you are the exception. Poverty creates lives so difficult that the remarkable thing is when a person actually manages to hold it all together.

My arrival in the inner city, then, came as something of a shock. If you have ever stayed in a chalet in a holiday camp – the type that has 'redcoats' – then you will know what I mean when I say you can hear everything that is going on next door. My small 'two up, two down' terrace became my castle, except that it wasn't much of a castle. The door from the front room opened right onto the pavement and the 'grounds' amounted to a pathway just wide enough to house a wheelie bin. The neighbours' doors were so close you could knock on them without leaving your own house. In Darkest England you cannot remain anonymous or hide yourself away for long – you get noticed, people talk to you, and children play in the street because there is no private space. Many sunny mornings Hannah and I sat on our front step eating breakfast, but we never noticed a stream of people off to work, no suits or briefcases walking down the street – more likely pyjamas and slippers.

If the mornings were quiet in our new community then the night-times were action-packed. Watching out of the bedroom window as a real live soap opera is played out is something that has to be experienced to be believed. My new neighbours included a drug dealer, several users, a man who had been convicted of an undisclosed crime for which he served a 22-year prison sentence, sex workers, a former Conservative party councillor, alcoholics, illegal immigrants, victims and proponents of domestic violence ... all these within the dozen houses around ours – or, within 40 metres of our front door.

A few days after I moved to Openshaw I heard a commotion in the street. When I looked out of the window, two grown men were fighting right outside my house and a crowd was gathering. It was the middle of the day, and one man was wearing a tracksuit, with the other in just a pair of shorts. I had never seen fighting like it except on TV and this was a whole lot more frightening. The fight somehow progressed into the house opposite, the two men still slogging it out as the crowd followed them into the house. Suddenly, through the crowd burst the man in the tracksuit running for his life, followed by the other man, still in just his shorts, brandishing a large kitchen knife. The brawlers sprinted off and I presume that my knife-wielding neighbour never caught up with his opponent.

I prayed earnestly to God that day – 'please don't let me die, not here, not now'. As I was getting ready for bed one night I heard what sounded like someone hitting a very low tom-tom drum very, very loudly. Looking out of the back window this time, I saw a car being driven at high speed by joyriders through the narrow alley, sending wheelie bins flying into the air every few feet. With sparks firing off both sides of the car as they scraped our back walls, and domestic rubbish flying everywhere, it was a kind of urban firework display.

Everything is different here. Over 30 per cent of the housing is empty; in some places entire streets are boarded up, and in others the bulldozers have already moved in to obliterate the 100-year-old terraced houses from the face of our community. There is an eerie sense of inappropriateness as you peer inside these tiny dwellings, looted for everything of worth and left exposed to the elements. The ruined shells of houses that were once the castles of mill workers seem to sing a haunting song of life, hard work and community living. Perhaps their imminent demise conjures up a romantic perception that things were better back then, when work was plentiful; when family life was more secure; when bunting adorned the narrow streets for the Queen's Coronation and for wartime celebrations; when street parties were common; when cars were only rarely seen. I feel sure that some things really were better then, and others just seem better after 40 or 50 years of forgetfulness to help numb the cold pain which surely existed in these streets back then too.

100 YEARS ON

In Booth's book he exposes the desperate plight of what he calls 'the submerged tenth': the 10 per cent of the population who, unseen by the majority, lived in conditions worse than that of London cab horses. He records story after story of people who are literally dying of starvation on the streets of England, men whose quest for work has been terminally fruitless, girls who have been lured into lives of prostitution, children who are 'not so much born into this world as damned into it'.[1] The gut-wrenching accounts, many transcribed from the record books of Salvation Army Rescue Homes, paint a horrific picture of life in the margins of Victorian England. The most pressing issues of the day for Booth were unemployment, homelessness, poverty, alcoholism and prostitution.[2] People in such circumstances, Booth concedes, are faced with a terrible choice – 'starve or steal'.

His deep compassion for those trapped in Darkest England is evident throughout his writing, and nowhere more so than in relaying the story of a man who walked from Liverpool to London, going without food for five days or more. The man died on his way to hospital and the coroner announced a verdict of death by starvation. He writes, '[Anyone who has] experienced the sinking sensation that is felt when even one meal has been sacrificed may form some idea of what kind of slow torture killed that man.' The harrowing accounts of girls who have been driven, bullied and seduced into prostitution are a chilling reminder of the harsh reality of the streets. A suicide note from a husband and father whose suicide pact failed is a disturbing insight into the desperation that can come over a person when every attempt to find work has failed and the daily struggle to put bread on the table has been continually futile.

Booth argued that the very minimum people deserved was to be treated as well as a cab horse. He says that if a cab horse stumbles and falls, 'weary or careless or stupid', 'there is no question of debate how he came to stumble before we try to get him on his legs again'.[3] For these horses there is no time or need to discuss the reason for their stumble, and yet when we see a brother or sister who is struggling to make life work properly, who has become homeless, jobless or addicted, our first desire is often to assess their credibility for help and ask 'are they worthy of my attention?' Booth argues that these working beasts are better cared for by society than the 3 million men, women and children he called a 'vast despairing multitude' who live in poverty. The horses are at least adequately fed and housed, cared for through sickness and given the dignity of an honest day's work, which seemed a far better deal than what Booth experienced in the pre-welfare-state slums of England at the turn of the twentieth century.

Then, just as is the case now, there was little by way of reliable data to confirm or oppose Booth's observation. He was working on broad figures from his own experience, and in England today we are no better off in this regard. Just how many people are addicts or alcoholics? How many illegal immigrants live on these shores with no source of legitimate income, forced to work for pitiful pay and unprotected by employment legislation? How many children are caring for parents at home – not just the sick but the addicted?

How much of the money paid out to individuals in welfare benefit finds its way into the hands of loan sharks, drug dealers and gang lords? We may never know the answers to some of these questions, but I can promise you that that such people and such circumstances exist, and you can meet them every day in Darkest England.

Booth saw the relative merits of educating the young, although he questions the validity of forcing one type of education on all types of child. 'Educated the children are not,' he moans. 'They are pressed through standards which exact a certain acquaintance with ABC ...'.[4]

His complaint was against the overbearing insistence on bundling all children together to pass through the same academic process for the same ultimate prize. To Booth, this was not only unfair on the poorer classes, whose nutrition and home circumstances would land them at a disadvantage, but would also lead to huge voids in the development of many of the skills necessary to make one's life (and indeed society) function properly. Over 100 years on, Booth would not be out of place making this argument at a meeting of the education authorities and youth service providers in England today, neither would he be alone in making his plea to the government officials who are charged with the responsibility of educating our children. 'Education is the new welfare' seems to be the message, but this alone will not be enough to rescue the children who are growing up in the margins of society.

The Labour Party mantra, 'Education, Education, Education!', suggests support for the presupposition that an increase in academic achievement will cure the ills of our society, but even if that were partly true it certainly isn't so in Darkest England, where vast numbers of children do not attend school. Many are permanently excluded for their inability to adapt to the behavioural code of the institution, others through their failure to attain consistent levels of work. Dozens of young people in our community simply do not attend school, and when there is no resistance from home and little incentive from school, a few days of unchallenged truancy have turned into weeks, months and years of absence. The schools do not seem to try especially hard to reintegrate troublesome teenagers; in fact in our experience they often actively discourage their return to school.

Take Sarah, for example: a 13-year-old with a troubled home life who repeatedly rebelled against the behavioural boundaries imposed by her school and consequently found herself suspended. Her mother, Lucy, was invited to attend a meeting at the school to discuss the issue and plan a return to school, but Lucy couldn't face such a meeting so, although she wanted to go back, Sarah never returned to school. After a year of absence the school are now suggesting that she finds another educational establishment to finish her education, but the education authorities will not even consider finding her another place because she is still registered at her original school. This process keeps the school's permanent exclusion quota low while removing Sarah and others like her from the classroom. Despite many attempts by Lucy and by us to find a way to 'jolt' the system from its nauseating inadequacy, Sarah remains permanently absent from school, with self-esteem and potential ebbing away slowly and forcefully.

This flaw in the system is consistently blamed on the pupil's inability to behave or achieve, and the child's inadequacies are once again paraded and used as a scapegoat. At some point there must come an acknowledgement that the education system is the inadequate party and a confession that schools themselves are at least as ineffectual at educating certain types of young people as the young people are unable to observe the institutional protocol.

As part of our mentoring programme, Sarah recently spent a whole morning in our church kitchen preparing a meal. Each stage was meticulously observed by her assessor, and with hygienic preparation and skilful design, the meal was cooked to perfection and nicely presented on the plate. Then arrived the guest of honour: Lucy, her mum, and the two of them sat together at a beautifully laid table and ate this feast before Sarah completed the final task of cleaning up. Sarah's reward will not so much be in the certificate that she will receive from the Unit Award Scheme but in the proud eyes of a mother who, for the first time in over a year, had seen her daughter fulfilling a tiny measure of the potential that she's been given.

FACES AND FIGURES

We live in a time of great change. Writer Douglas Rushkoff has said, 'Without having migrated a single inch, we have nevertheless travelled further than any generation in history.'[5] Culture has shifted beyond recognition in so many ways over the last century: two world wars have come and gone, travel – both local and foreign – has become a normality, the birth of rock and roll and the media invention of the teenager have all changed our lives for ever.

Technology has taken over, with computers, the information superhighway, mobiles, email and text messaging being a part of everyday life for most of us. And yet, in spite of such change, it seems that one thing remains consistent: the levels of people living in poverty in the UK. The most recent figures regarding poverty in the UK, make for disturbing reading. A staggering one in five people are said to be living in poverty in the UK. That amounts to 13 million people, children are one and a third times more likely to live in low income households than adults. This figure is double what it read at the end of the 1970s and is four times Booth's estimated 3 million.[6] Contrary to common perception, the gap between rich and poor has become larger over the last decade. In the last 15 years more households have become poor, and already wealthy areas have tended to become disproportionately wealthier.

In some areas of our cities over half of all households are breadline poor.[7] The poorest tenth of the UK's population share between them just 2 per cent of the UK's total income. The majority of people falling into this category are, perhaps surprisingly, working-age adults without children or couples with children. Relatively few are either lone parents or pensioners.

We can see the concentration of poverty when looking at statistics regarding free school meals: half of the primary school children who are entitled to free school meals are concentrated in one-fifth of the schools.[8] This means that although there is increased social and geographic mobility, the poor are mainly living in pockets the rich can generally avoid. Despite a fairly robust governmental policy for the eradication of child poverty, the introduction of additional benefits for pensioners and working families, and initiatives like SureStart and New Deal for Communities, lots more still needs to be done as little impact seems to have been made on the number of people living below the poverty line.

What the above statistics tell us is that the problem of poverty is not limited to a handful of people consigned to living in squalid conditions in a tower block somewhere, or to the alcoholic, drug-using community. The figures are too high for that. Neither could we claim that 'it is their own doing', as if people would choose a lifestyle of poverty for all its attractions. Poverty is widespread and exists in all kinds of communities for all kinds of reasons, and it crushes the spirit of an individual.

Debbie is a mum – a very good mum, who cares for her two boys really well. Debbie is also a daughter – a very good daughter, caring for her sick mother who lives two miles away and sometimes needs two visits each day. Debbie doesn't get much money but she makes sure there is enough to clothe the boys and eat most days and sometimes get the bus to Mum's if it is raining really hard. She has never had need of a passport and she doesn't have a driving licence; foreign travel and owning a car are not things that she would view as ever likely to be part of her life. She couldn't go anywhere anyway because her Mum is dependent on her. Debbie wanted to open a bank account but you need ID to do that so they would only give her a very basic account that can only be accessed at the branch – meaning more bus fares, more hours of lugging the kids around just to move money in and out of the bank.

One day early in January, after a typically frugal Christmas, a man knocked on the door and offered Debbie membership of a Christmas savings club. He said he would call each week to collect her savings and then at Christmas she would have the joy of really splashing out on the kids and having a Christmas like she'd always dreamed of. She duly signed up and sure enough the man visited, come rain or shine, to collect her Christmas savings. In October 2006 Farepak, the company who this man worked for, declared their bankruptcy and issued a statement to customers saying that there would be no return on their investment. Like thousands of others in my community, and probably in yours, Debbie lost hundreds of pounds, her dream Christmas and her faith in humanity. It is not only the foolish, the hedonistic, the addicted or the lazy who suffer.

In each stage of life, from birth to death, the effects of poverty are evident. The infant mortality rate among children whose parents are in unskilled or semi-skilled work is one and a half times that of children born to managers and professionals. Babies from poorer households are also more likely to have a low birth weight. A child of secondary school age with parents in routine employment is less than half as likely to achieve five GCSEs at grade C or above. Young men in unskilled work are three times more likely to commit suicide than those in more qualified positions. Poverty also increases a person's chance of suffering from mental illness – the poorest fifth of the population are more than twice as likely to be affected by this than those in the richer classes. A person employed in unskilled or semi-skilled work is more than twice as likely to die from heart disease or lung cancer, and also has double the probability of having a limiting long-standing illness or disability by the age of 45.

A quarter of people on low income have either no freezer or no washing machine, but despite their lack of valuable assets they are three times more likely to have their houses burgled. The irony of this is that half of the most vulnerable households have no house insurance, so when disaster does strike there is no backup or chance of replacing whatever has been damaged or stolen.[8]

The statistics reveal only part of the truth. From the politician's office, the researcher's desk, the viewer's armchair and the church's pews it is hard to taste the desperate hardship that they describe. It is one thing to look at a graph which indicates that the child mortality rate is higher in areas of urban deprivation than in affluent suburban communities, but it is quite another to sit with a mother who has just buried her third child as she clings tightly to the one who lives on, or to sense the grief of a father whose teenage daughter's life was abruptly ended when she was attacked with a broken bottle. It is easy to pass judgement when a newsreader informs us of the death of 'another' drug addict, the son of a city which nurtured him, then robbed him of all his self-worth and left him to rot for two weeks in a squat before anyone noticed he was missing, but when that young man is a friend, a father, a son who shared his broken life with so many, the news cuts like a knife into the stomach of those who loved and lost. It may be fascinating to learn that health and dental care in Darkest England is significantly worse than other areas but when a teenager is moaning in the next room because of toothache, having never been taken to the dentist, popping handfuls of painkillers just to get through the day, the statistics become a reality, not figures to be observed but needs to be met.

'Our own research suggests that non-poor people can hold powerful negative stereotypes of the "undeserving poor", have difficulty with the concept of relative poverty in an affluent society and have little understanding of the way in which poverty affects life chances. We thus need a revolution in empathy.'[9]

The Fabian Society

References and Notes

1. Booth, p. 40.
2. Booth, p. 15.
3. Booth, p. 15.
4. Booth, p. 13.
5. Rushkoff, D., *Children of Chaos* (Flamingo, 1997), p. 3.
6. The Joseph Rowntree Foundation, Monitoring poverty and social exclusion, 2007, summary on www.poverty.org.uk,
7. The Joseph Rowntree Foundation, Poverty, Wealth and Place in Britain, 1968–2005.
8. The Joseph Rowntree Foundation, Monitoring poverty and social exclusion, 2005, www.poverty.org.uk.
9. The Fabian Society 'Narrowing the Gap' Executive Summary, 2006.

.2

GOOD NEWS TO THE POOR IS – 'YOU AIN'T POOR NO MORE!'

General Booth's writing contains the implicit notion that all Salvationists and all readers of the book would already have accepted that they have a God-given responsibility to serve the poor. There is little by way of explanation or specific call to this; rather, it is just assumed that Christians reading his proposals would be actively seeking out ways to engage with the underclasses and minister to them.

Perhaps this was true, and on the threshold of the twentieth century the church was well motivated to work in such areas, or perhaps it was Booth's evidently idealistic outlook that allowed him to presume such conviction. Either way, what I do know is that today it would not be wise to make such an assumption.

I regularly teach a seminar for a group of gap year students on the subject 'God's heart for the poor', and every time I discover that the majority of students are from good church backgrounds and are intelligent, passionate, servant-hearted young people, but they have never been taught anything on this subject before. They, like many Christians I meet today, have been taught a theology which deprives God of one of his primary characteristics – his concern for the poor.

George Bernard Shaw said, 'God made man in his own image – and we have decided to return the favour.' It is all too easy to make the Gospel what we'd like it to be and to make God into a god that looks a lot like us by misrepresenting scripture and by effectively removing the bits that we find difficult.

It would also be easy for you to skip the rest of this chapter if it starts to get uncomfortable, but it's absolutely central to everything else in the book, so I urge you to stick with it.

FACE VALUE

When our son Joel was born I decided to reduce my hours working as a pastor so that I could take care of him for two days each week while Hannah returned to work. During that time I noticed a stark contrast in the way new people responded to me depending on how I introduced myself, especially if I arrived somewhere to teach a leadership seminar or deliver some training and I introduced myself as a house husband. Perhaps it was in my imagination, but it often felt as though people's expectations just dropped through the floor.

My role in life very much affects people's opinion of my value. If my seminar defied the dwindling expectation of the audience then I could regain that value by demonstrating my skill, and the price tag I've been assigned may be overwritten with a more satisfying figure.

Psychologists tell us that we value people in four key ways:

1. **What they do**
2. **What they look like**
3. **What they have**
4. **What skills they have**

Our current cultural obsession with the beautiful, talented celebrities of the sports field, the music industry and the film screen does nothing to disprove their theory, and neither does our own attitude and experience if we are really, brutally honest.

Perhaps it's unfair to tar you with the same brush as I reluctantly use on myself, but I know that however wrong it looks when I write it down I have a tendency to use these criteria myself and I know I am judged by others in the same way. The truth is not just that we use these four criteria to make judgements about a person's value but that in our consumer society a person's wealth is almost always the key factor in the way that we perceive them.

Some years ago I spent a few short days in Johannesburg, South Africa, and visited the Ethembeni Aids Orphanage, which is run by the Salvation Army. During my time there I cared for a beautiful baby boy called Tumi who affected me so deeply that I still speak of him regularly nearly ten years on. He was about 9 months old and his head was the size of two heads because his mother drank so heavily during her pregnancy. She later left him on a rubbish dump, where he was rescued by the Army. Tumi had no possessions – even the tiny babygrows which he wore each day of his tragic life did not belong to him, and he couldn't call a single toy his own. He had no prospects of ever doing anything, such was the level of brain damage which he had sustained. He had no hope even of adoption or finding a family to take him in because he was so disfigured and his needs were so great.

But he did have something: he had eyes that recognised my sadness and said 'it's OK' as he blessed me hour after hour with his simple smile and knowing eyes. In those days my pathetic western value system was obliterated as I saw the value of human life, and regardless of the psychologists' criteria, perhaps for a second I saw humanity as God sees us, valuable because we exist. James 2:1–6 challenges everything within us that has a tendency towards judging people, especially in relation to their material possessions, and specifically forbids the favouring of the rich above the poor, saying, 'Has not God chosen those who are poor in the eyes of the world to be rich in faith and to inherit the kingdom he promised those who love him? But you have insulted the poor.'

'The poor' matter. Our culture may say different, the world may say it is acceptable that 50,000 people, including 30,000 children, die in Africa each day from preventable diseases; society may say that the illegal trafficking of young boys and girls for prostitution and slavery is not a high enough priority for them to tackle; we may convince ourselves that buying clothes which have been stitched by the hands of Eastern European women and children who spend every day in terrible working conditions is a good bargain. We may think that the body fished out of the canal was just another lowlife, tramp or junkie but the Bible says different – it says that like Tumi, each one matters, each one is loved, each one is valuable because they exist.

WHAT THE BIBLE HAS TO SAY ABOUT THE POOR

In their book *Lift the Label*,[1] David Westlake and Esther Stansfield offer this revealing walk through the Bible to highlight the centrality of the poor throughout the whole of scripture.

> From the first time God reveals himself to his chosen people, a slave nation, he identifies himself as a compassionate God who actively intervenes to liberate the poor and oppressed so that his people can worship him. Throughout Leviticus and Deuteronomy God sets up a legal system and structures designed to protect the needs and uphold the rights of the poor and needy.

> God's passion for justice for the poor resonates through the prophets Amos and Micah, through whom God warns people that they will be punished if they don't look after the vulnerable and the weak. The fulfilment of this prophecy in the splitting of the Israelite nation is a sober reminder of the importance that God attached to the treatment of the poor.

> In the Psalms and Proverbs a portrait is painted of a God who not only judges those who fail to act to help the poor but the one who is so moved by love and compassion that he takes action himself to bring hope to those in despair.

In Isaiah we are told of the one who will come to 'preach good news to the poor ... to bind up the broken-hearted, to proclaim freedom for the captives and release from darkness for prisoners' (Is 61:1). In the Gospels we read about Jesus, the one who personifies justice, love and compassion – the radical servant king. He touches the untouchables, eats with the outsiders, heals the sick and preaches good news to the poor.

Westlake claims that if you were to remove every page on which you found some mention of the poor from the Bible then its weight would be reduced so much that it would no longer stand on its end – a very plausible claim when you consider that there are over 800 references to the poor throughout the Old and New Testaments. But it is not just the volume of comments about the poor that command our attention, it is the content, and in some cases the ferocity of the words and actions of God against those who do nothing to relieve the suffering of the poor.

WORTHLESS WORSHIP – TWO EXAMPLES

'Amos' – the name itself means 'burdened', and any reading of his book leaves you in no doubt that he knew something of the burden God has for the marginalised and oppressed. He also bore the burden of announcing to his own people the dissatisfaction of their God. This calling would not win him any friends. Dated at around 760 BC, the prophecies of Amos foretold the certainty of judgement on the nations surrounding Israel and on Israel itself because of, among other things, the inappropriateness of their worship and sacrifices when their lifestyle did not match up (4:4, 5). Amos 5:21, where it says, 'I hate, I despise your religious feasts; I cannot stand your assemblies' gives you a flavour of the intensity with which Amos delivered his message from the Lord, and just a few verses earlier we can read why God was not impressed by the great feasts and festivals which ran for days and days: 'You trample on the poor and force him to give you grain' (5:11). In a nutshell God says through Amos: all the while you are responsible for causing poverty and oppression, or even if you are just too selfish to do anything about it, then don't bring your worship to me because it sounds like a racket!

Similarly in the book of Isaiah the prophet challenges the insincerity of worship: '. . . on the day of your fasting, you do as you please' (58:3b). He goes on to say that you cannot expect your voice to be heard on high if there is all manner of quarrelling, violence, injustice and oppression going on; if these things remain part of your lives then your words (however poetic), your songs (however tuneful), and your sacrifices (however fragrant) are hollow and meaningless to his ears. What then would the God of the universe have us offer to him in our worship? What would be pleasing to him?

'Is not this the kind of fasting I have chosen: to loose the chains of injustice and untie the cords of the yoke, to set the oppressed free and break every yoke? Is it not to share your food with the hungry and to provide the poor wanderer with shelter – when you see the naked, to clothe him' Isaiah 58:6, 7.

It hardly seems possible in the light of such clear scriptural instruction that in much of the church we remain unstirred by the reality of life for the poor, not just in our own communities but right across the world. We continue to elevate the performer, and just like the first hearers of the prophecies of Amos and Isaiah we turn worship into a showpiece in the naïve belief that God is interested. There is much debate around the church about styles of worship – traditional versus contemporary seems to be the great divide in many churches – and all the time we are digging our heels into whichever trench we happen to be standing in, we are avoiding the real question, the question on the heart of the one who we worship – 'what did you do for the poor?' It's not that

God doesn't want to be worshipped (it seems clear throughout scripture that worship is our primary purpose for existence), it's just that whether you strum it, blow down it or jump up and down on it God's first question is: what is your response to the poor and the oppressed? And it is your answer to that question that determines whether the sound that you make is pleasing to the one person in the audience that really matters.

Perhaps this story about a friend is an example of the kind of worship God enjoys. Chris had spent the weekend ferrying boxes to and fro in his car as he moved into his new house (you very rarely see removal vans in Darkest England, people's possessions are generally carted in open-booted cars, shopping trolleys, wheelie bins, or for the wealthier nomad – a Transit van). He returned to work at the Eden office on Monday morning suitably excited about having got one foot firmly planted on the property ladder. At lunchtime he made the few hundred metre dash back to his new bachelor pad, expecting to continue unpacking the assorted cardboard boxes that are associated with any house move.

Arriving home, he discovered that his new house had been burgled and stripped of everything of any value. Typically resourceful, Chris decided to go knocking on the neighbours' doors wondering if anyone had seen anything 'suspicious', such as someone making off with the entire contents of his house in the middle of the day! The door of the house immediately next door was ajar, so he wandered inside only to discover all his belongings sitting there in the front room. No-one seemed to be in the house so Chris, with the help of two policemen who he had flagged down, began taking all the items which belonged to him back to their rightful home.

The few months that followed these bizarre events tell a remarkable story of servanthood and grace. Chris was understandably terrified about the potential repercussions of this event. Would the neighbour return with a crew of thuggish mates to repossess their loot? Would they want to silence him to prevent their conviction in court? Would they one day return to borrow a cup of sugar and take the TV and Playstation by mistake? Nevertheless he confronted the neighbour, Steve, and although he never apologised or admitted involvement in the burglary there came a sort of unspoken understanding between the two men. In fact Steve offered to look after Chris's garden for him as a sort of payback.

As their relationship developed it became apparent that Steve was a drug user and was extremely unwell. Chris was able to support him through many tough times and try to encourage him in his struggle to stay sober and drug free, a struggle in which Steve was never victorious. As his health worsened Steve often had to go for long spells in hospital for dialysis and Chris began to visit him during those stays. They would talk about all kinds of things, but crucially Chris was able to share the good news of Jesus with him in those visits – a message which I know would have been easy to believe when he had seen the love of God and the effects of forgiveness all around since meeting the messenger. As well as visits from Chris, my wife Hannah nursed Steve in hospital for a short while and was able to get to know him a little bit before his liver finally gave up and he died in Manchester Royal Infirmary.

During his time in Openshaw, and now as Chris continues his work in another tough neighbourhood, I believe that the way God's ears are tuned, Chris has a fine voice for worship. Not because he is Russell Watson or Robbie Williams, but because his heart reflects the heart of God and his hands do the work of God in releasing the oppressed and being good news to the poor. Today, just as in the time of Amos and Isaiah, God is blessed by the worship that we demonstrate with our lives, not just what we sing.

GOD IDENTIFIES HIMSELF WITH THE POOR

It is not just that God is bothered about poverty and oppression like a concerned onlooker. There is a sense as we read the Old and New Testaments that God actually identifies himself with the poor. Proverbs 17:5 says, 'He who mocks the poor shows contempt for their Maker', as if somehow the passer-by that hurls abuse at a tramp who sleeps on a bench in your local park actually insults God, or that the bullies who taunt the kid from the estate because he doesn't have the right trainers cause offence to the creator of the universe.

In Matthew 25 Jesus himself is recorded as saying, 'I tell you the truth, whatever you did for one of the least of these brothers of mine, you did for me.' Again Jesus puts himself on the receiving end of our actions towards one another, and this time he specifically mentions being fed, befriended, clothed and visited. He spells out to us that our actions towards those in such poverty, whether generous or miserly, are done to the Saviour himself and will reap the rewards accordingly.

Mother Theresa of Calcutta claimed that her great gift was 'to see the face of Jesus in its most distressing disguise'. She had the ability to look at a person ravaged with disease and infection or suffering after terrible brutality and see in them the face of Jesus. This gift surely enabled her to spend her life as she did, selflessly poured out on behalf of the poor.

There seems little doubt then that God sides with the poor, and to a large extent God could justifiably identify himself as 'poor'. Jesus' own experiences here on earth were almost entirely the kind of experiences associated with the poor. He was born in squalid conditions, of questionable parentage, a refugee, an outcast, with no place to lay his head, living on the margins of society, the victim of abuse and injustice, and executed in the most demeaning, undignified fashion. However, it is often argued (usually by wealthier Christians) that surely God can't be prejudiced in his benevolence towards the poor – God must love us all equally. To some extent this is a valid argument, but it is not that the poor are somehow more deserving because of their lack of resources. In fact, God is a God of justice, and all the while the poor are oppressed he will stand against the oppressor on the side of the poor. As Vinoth Ramachandra has said, 'in a sinful world where life is biased towards the wealthy and the powerful, God's actions will always be perceived as a counter bias'.[2]

WHO ARE 'THE POOR'?

I don't know too many people who would be eager to call themselves rich. We have a tendency to feel hard up when we are not able to afford a foreign holiday or we have to buy a cheaper brand of coffee, but in God's eyes these are not the things that make us poor. In the Old Testament, several Hebrew words are used in reference to the poor: *anaw*, *ani*, *dal*, *ebyon* and *ras*. Together they create an image of a person who is weak, thin, wrongfully made poor, and/or dependent. In the New Testament, just one Greek word is used for the same purpose – *ptochos* means someone whose life is in ruins and must accept help from other people.[3]

Throughout the Bible, these terms are used to describe widows, orphans, the sick and beggars. The poor are those who for some reason cannot make their lives work properly without help from someone else and it is easy to identify such people in our society today. This could happen for any number of reasons, and here are two examples.

Any day of the week after 3:30, our office and small hall is in chaos. Young people dropping in on their way home from school, groups coming in for their mentoring sessions, workers getting ready for after-school dance clubs or kids' club. It is a noisy hub of life in the middle of our community. One day a lad came in looking rather upset and asked if he could show us something, so we found a quiet corner and David pulled from his pocket a crumpled picture of himself being violently abused by his Dad. He told us that his Dad regularly did this and his mates took pictures for fun. David was poor, a 13-year-old trapped in a terrible prison of abuse from which he could not escape. He needed help. Working with the other agencies in our community we were able to help David to safety and we continue to support him in building some sort of life for himself.

Tracey has a baby daughter and is trying her best to face all the challenges of parenthood, but however hard she tries she always runs out of nappies and baby milk before the end of the week. They are so expensive in the corner shop but she has no way of getting to the out-of-town superstores. Tracey is poor – she is trying to get it right but she cannot starve her baby and leave her unchanged for 48 hours until her next giro comes in, so we keep a stock of nappies and milk in our house and when she runs out she brings the baby to our house to get clean and fed.

CONSUMER CULTURE

As Christians in the twenty-first-century western world we have a great challenge on our hands. We exist in a world which is defined by materialism, by the incessant gathering of possessions. I regularly drive past the Trafford Centre in Manchester with its huge mosque-like domes imposing on the skyline in an unashamed architectural claim to clerical significance. Such 'temples' have become places of pilgrimage for the devoted consumer. Shopping has become a major leisure pursuit for many people, and while creativity once meant 'what I can make', it has come to mean 'what I can buy'.

If you ever venture into your local shopping centre on a Saturday afternoon you will encounter a frenzied mass of people laden with bags full of items they don't need, paid for with money they don't have, in order to maintain the appearance of a lifestyle they can't afford. The consumer is not only concerned with having enough, but is an indulgent creature that constantly craves more.

The idea that once upon a time people only bought new shoes or new trousers when their old pair got worn out is something that the children of our current age find inconceivable. Whether it is computer games, phones or fashion for the young, or a bigger car, exotic holidays and home improvements for the more mature consumer, we are all affected by the advertisers' lie that somehow life will be better if we upgrade our gadgets or renew our wardrobe. Marketing moguls sell us discontentment every day and they do a great job of it.

Consumerism is at its height at Christmas-time, the great annual opportunity for us to celebrate something of eternal significance. Immanuel, God with us, has become a time associated with shopping and spending. Every year consumers in the UK spend a whopping 156 million pounds on 3 million Christmas trees to decorate their homes, they also spend 30 million pounds on brussell sprouts as well as felling 200,000 trees which are made into Christmas cards.[4] The average amount of money spent per family on Christmas Day, not including presents, is £564. Adding together all the costs of the season including clothes, food, drink, parties, presents and travel comes to £862 per person in the country. According to Switch, the debit card company, this amount has risen by around 20 per cent in the last six years.

These figures, of course, drop significantly among low-income families; a family of four who live on benefits are estimated to spend £121 between them over the whole Christmas season. Despite only half of us in the UK holding any kind of savings we rack up 10 billion pounds of debt at Christmas in our annual credit card bonanza. In consumer Britain we are more likely to be gathered around the 'hole in the wall' than the baby in the manger at Christmas.[5]

The Farepak Christmas Savings company, which promised a Christmas to remember, certainly delivered on that promise when in October 2006, having collected 40 million pounds of savings from one hundred and fifty thousand people, they announced that they were going into liquidation. They told their customers that they might retrieve as little as 4 per cent of their investment. Typically the majority of Farepak savers were from working-class communities, the sort of people who don't have bank accounts or transport and used this facility because they are conscientious and organised and wanted the best for their families. They actually got a Christmas of misery instead of joy.

Meanwhile the chairman of Farepak takes a pre-Christmas break in Argentina and is shown on TV leaving a five-star hotel in Buenos Aires refusing to talk to the cameras. Once again the rich oppress the poor and force them to hand over 'grain' – it's not so different to Amos' time after all. It is true that money will not solve every problem that exists where people are poor but we can be certain from the Bible that God cares, and if that is true then we have a great responsibility to act to demonstrate that care. Micah 6:8 says, 'He has showed you, O man, what is good. And what does the LORD require of you? To act justly and to love mercy and to walk humbly with your God.'

The problem with culture is that it pervades all aspects of society including the church and in truth the church has put up little resistance to the onslaught of consumerism. Over the last 50 years we have expended endless amounts of energy battling on all kinds of other fronts in order to maintain our moral distinctive; meanwhile materialism and consumerism have slipped unannounced into the Christian community and without warning taken a foothold in the lives of many a disciple who, unstirred even by their own conscience, has dethroned the God of the universe to make way for our cultural deity of materialism. No longer are their lives directed by the heartfelt leading of the Spirit or by the reading of scripture or by the needs of the poor in their own neighbourhood, instead they are now slaves to the desire to maximise spending power. Mammon is, as Ambrose Bierce has put it, 'the god of the world's leading religion'.

OUR RESPONSE

In order to find its way back into Darkest England the church must once again acknowledge its God-given mandate to serve the poor and stand up for the oppressed. This is not, and can never be, purely the domain of those believers who 'are that way inclined' or to those who 'feel a particular burden for the poor'; a commitment to the poor is integral to the Christian faith, paramount in the teaching of Jesus and inherently part of the character of God and therefore any serious follower of Jesus must take seriously their responsibility to the poor.

Firstly we must learn to repent of our aspirations for wealth. It does seem ironic that in light of all that scripture says about God being among the poor, we still seem more intent on mimicking the rich in our lifestyles. The things around us so easily draw us in and it is a constant battle to remain focused on God's values and reject those of the world. For many of us it is not only that we have neglected our responsibility to those in the margins of society, living lives entirely detached from the underclasses, but that we have also spent time complaining about all the things that we do not have, disappointed that we cannot afford that new car, new shoes or a night out.

We are guilty of feigning poverty when in actual fact we are among the wealthiest people on the planet;[6] this can be nothing more than an offensive racket of ungrateful children in the ears of God. We need to make a conscious effort to have grateful hearts, to live simple lives, to hold our possessions lightly and with open hands, always offering what we have back to God and to those in need. This will breed in us a generous spirit which is open to giving and receiving, and begin to release us from the 'monster of more'.

As one theologian has said, 'we need to reduce the distance between ourselves and the poor'. That means finding out where the needs are in your community and walking towards them. Whether it is among lonely pensioners, young families, vulnerable children or young people does not matter – what matters is that we involve ourselves in the lives of those who are struggling to make their lives work properly.

We will look at this in depth in the next chapter but there is a great need for Christians to search out the toughest corners of the land and go and make our nests there, modelling community and family, experiencing first hand what it is like to live in an area crippled by unemployment, crime and poverty. We have seen that God is concerned about those on the margins of our society, but the primary way that people will see that concern is through the actions of God's people.

We will need to lovingly confront materialism in our brother and sister when we see it. This will be tough because money has become something of a taboo in the church. We don't discuss how much we earn or spend very openly. It is said that during the Crusades men were baptised by full immersion but held their swords out of the water, and it could be said that the same is true of western Christians, except that in our case we hold our wallets out of the water. If there is one thing that we resist giving God total control of it is our wallets and that must change if we are to return to Darkest England. The gods of mammon and materialism must be dethroned in our churches because we cannot serve two masters, and God must be God of the church. Neil Hannon from the band Divine Comedy penned the following song lyrics, which offer us a pertinent insight into how the church is perceived by the world outside. I'll leave you to decide if he has a point.

> 'The cars in the churchyard are shiny and German
> Distinctly at odds with the theme of the sermon
> And during communion I study the people
> Squeezing themselves through the eye of the needle.'[7]
>
> **Neil Hannon**

References and Notes

1. Westlake, D. and Stansfield, E., *Lift the Label* (Authentic, 2005), pp. 64–5.
2. Ramachandra, V., in Chester, T. *Good News to the Poor* (Inter-Varsity Press, 2004), p. 19.
3. Westlake, D. and Borlase, C., *Upwardly Mobile: How to Live a Life of Spiritual Significance* (Hodder & Stoughton, 2000).
4. Xmas by numbers, 21/12/2006, Matt Roper, www.mirror.co.uk.
5. Roberts, Y., '£564 a family: the cost of Christmas Day', in *The Observer*, 15 December 2002.
6. *Lift the label* says that if you have a bank account you are in the richest 8 per cent of the world's population.
7. Hannon, N., of The Divine Comedy, 'Eye of the Needle' on the album *Regeneration*.

.3

Towards the end of *In Darkest England and The Way Out*, as Booth is summarising his thesis, he says that the reason that the Salvation Army was best placed to deliver the incredible plan that he laid out is because many early-day Salvationists were from these places. He says, 'They are in touch with them. They live in the same street, work in the same shops and factories, and come in contact with them at every turn and corner of life'.[1] According to Booth one of the unique things about the Army was that it recruited many of its members and officers from the 'submerged tenth', the underclasses. It took people who were uneducated and unskilled, in many cases addicted, destitute people, and gave them hope and something to live for. Booth was right that it would be of huge benefit when trying to reach out to poor people in poor communities for the majority of the workforce to be familiar with that lifestyle. This would surely make access to people, relationship building and credibility much more achievable than if he had approached the same task with personnel primarily recruited from the middle and upper classes.

However, I can't help feeling that for all the genius of Booth's proposal there is a weakness here in his long-term thinking. Shortly after he claims that many of his people are from the slums he says 'If they don't live amongst them, they formerly did'. Presumably having found salvation in Booth's Army, many had lifted themselves clear of their former lives and out of Darkest England altogether. He would, of course, see this as positive progress and betterment for the individual, and who could argue with that? The unemployed finding work, the alcoholic giving up the drink, the hungry being fed, the homeless being housed – but over time this process, repeated thousands of times, generation after generation, would result in the whole Army being upwardly mobile, in fact upwards and away from the people it was first called to.

MOVING OUT

One of my first jobs when I moved to Manchester was to have a meal with a couple who had kindly offered their support to us as we moved into Openshaw. We spent a delightful evening with Bob and Brenda Kyle in their lovely home, eating Brenda's amazing cooking and enjoying the warmth of their hospitality – in fact Hannah enjoyed it so much that she stayed there for three months before getting a house on the estate. Bob is a mechanical engineer and Brenda was a head teacher, both lovely, generous people, and it soon became apparent that they had a very personal reason for supporting our project.

Just around the corner from our house is the pub where Bob's grandfather Sam Kyle met the Salvation Army and ultimately his saviour. His testimony was that as a heavy drinker who could not read or write he sat at the bar listening as a young Salvationist girl sang the song 'A Light Came Out of The Darkness'. His attention was grabbed by the music and the words which washed over him and he was compelled to follow the band back to the hall. Captain Young was the Corps Officer and he spent time teaching Sam not just the basics of the Christian faith but also to read and write. Sam soon gave up the drink and joined the ranks of the Army and actually served as the Corps Sergeant Major of Higher Openshaw Corps for 49 years. This obviously had a major effect on his life and the life of his family, who found themselves with food on the table and a whole new focus for their lives. The next generation, having seen first hand the benefits of living Christian lives of self-control and commitment continued on in dedicated service in the Army, holding down good jobs and establishing a comfortable lifestyle. By the time Bob was born, opportunity beckoned – with a good home life, Christian values firmly established throughout the family, a supportive social network and the opportunity for education and lucrative employment, soon after he and Brenda were married they were able to move out of the fast declining community of Openshaw to pastures new. What an amazing testimony to the world that through the ministry of General Booth's Army a whole family, generation after generation, has been saved from lives of poverty. This is what *In Darkest England and The Way Out* is all about. How different their story could have been had those early-day Army saints not ventured into that pub.

Such has been the effectiveness of the Army's ministry over the years that Bob's story is by no means an isolated one. Recently a couple visited our Sunday morning meeting and in conversation with them we discovered that exactly 46 years previously they had been married in Openshaw Salvation Army. Having grown up around our estate they had gone off to become Salvation Army officers, travelled the world and lived in many different homes. Now living in York, they are spending their retirement far from the community where they spent their youth.

Over and over, generation after generation this has occurred and there has been little by way of response; very few people in comparison have made the socio-economic journey into these areas of deprivation. Little by little the Army has found itself detached from the underclasses consigned largely to the suburbs of Britain. At the dawn of the twenty-first century we find ourselves with something of an identity crisis, longing to have the impact and significance of the Army of old but with little or no connection to the darkest corners of the society in which we exist.

SA – GO HOME!

An important part of our journey back to Darkest England will be the conscious choice to relocate ourselves to communities where the poor are found in great numbers. There are many people doing good things in these communities: regeneration partnerships, youth services, social services, SureStart, and many more. However, these groups are staffed almost entirely by professionals who drive in to run their activities and programmes and then retreat to their homes in outlying districts at the end of the day.

That is not to say that there is no value in this kind of work – we have seen great achievements in some areas by some external campaigners – but there is a niche to which the church is called, a gap which, as far as I am aware, no other organisations are queuing up to fill, and that is the niche of incarnational living.

There is a need for people who will join with the poor in Darkest England and become part of these communities, making real friendships with people that may seem very different to us at the outset but allowing them to shape and change us so that we can become at home in their native territory.

For some of us this will be just as cross-cultural as if we had moved to another country, as we learn new customs, new values, get used to a new diet and in some cases a new language (not 'The Queen's English'). The Salvation Army has a great heritage of cross-cultural credibility. When Hannah's great-grandparents went as Salvation Army officers to India in the early 1900s they changed their names from Alfred and Edith Alistone to Ranjit Singh and Jeya Priti.

They left behind the black serge uniforms, preferring to wear traditional Indian clothing including turbans with 'The Salvation Army' emblazoned on them. Just as inspiring are those who did not travel across vast oceans to find their mission field: 'Slum Sisters' were Salvationists who chose to live in the East End Slums. Booth says of these 100 women: 'Some are ladies born and bred, who have not been afraid to exchange the comfort of a West End drawing room for service among the vilest of the vile, and a residence in small and fetid rooms whose walls were infested with vermin.'[2] He was so humbled by their work that he refused to report on it himself but instead offers an excerpt from the *New York World* which is a stunning account of what the reporter found when she visited these cross-cultural missionaries for a few days.

INCARNATIONAL GOD

We have an incarnational God. John 1:14 says, 'The Word became flesh and made his dwelling among us. We have seen his glory, the glory of the One and Only, who came from the Father, full of grace and truth.' The God we serve left all the glories of heaven, emptying himself of all outward glory (John 17:5, Phil 2:7) to become poor while remaining the fullness of God (Col 2:9). This is incarnation modeled by God himself through Christ. I have sometimes wondered why Jesus came to the earth.

Since I was a child I have been taught that he came to take onto himself the sins of humanity, but why did it need to happen here on earth when God has the whole of the cosmos to play with? Surely the sacrifice through which God's wrath was satisfied (according to one popular song) is worth the same whether meted out on earth or heaven or on the moon or on a star especially created for that purpose. There has to be more to it than that. God must have considered it to be of great importance for him to become flesh and walk amongst us for 33 years as a human being. There are many answers to this question and I want to give you just two:

1. Jesus being here on the earth helps us to understand who God is. We gain much of our understanding about the nature of God from the life and teachings of Jesus. Without the Gospel accounts our theological and personal understanding of God would be greatly diminished.

2. Jesus being here on earth demonstrates and bestows dignity on humanity. It lets us know that we are not worthless products of an evolutionary process with no purpose or value, whose lives are a mere grain of sand on a million beaches of eternity. We matter and someone cares.[3]

These two ideas help us to consider our own incarnational mandate. First, the church needs to be present in tough places in order to make God known. We are to be the 'visible echo of the invisible God'.[4] A worker in Fitton Hill, Oldham, once had 'Jesus lives 'ere' daubed on his front door by a local youth.

Needless to say that graffiti didn't get cleaned off for quite a while! In a very real sense, that person is a visible representation of God to his community – whenever people look at him they are reminded of what God is like, and if ever they wonder what God is like they can look at God's people to get an idea. If the church is absent from the great expanses of darkness throughout Britain, then how will they ever encounter the light?

Second, our presence in such places will remind people that they are valuable, worth bothering with. When our teams are out doing detached youth work the young people are somewhat bemused by their presence, especially when it's dark, cold and raining. The question often comes: 'What are you doing here?' and our answer is met with as much suspicion as our presence – we say, 'We've come to meet you.'

That is of course our only reason for being there, and somehow as we demonstrate in small ways that we value them enough to go out of our way to meet them, they come a little closer to knowing that there is a God who loves and values them. If the church does not think these people worthy of our company then they will presume that they are not worthy of God's attention either.

FIRST IMPRESSIONS

The day is marked indelibly on my brain: 23 September 1999. Not my wedding anniversary, baptism or child's birthday but the first day I came to Manchester. The call to relocate to Darkest England is a tough one, and I personally wouldn't budge without a fight. It was a grey, rainy day which had somehow gone from being a 'visit' with a friend to being a job interview for the role of EDEN team leader at Openshaw – a post for which I genuinely do not remember applying. As the only candidate in the waiting room and ultimately the only one to enter the interview room, my sad attempts to express lethargy towards the project and my own personal incompetence were in vain and I left the Salvation Army headquarters with a job offer in hand and a feeling that my entire future was ebbing away before my eyes. That was of course exactly what was happening.

A short car journey took us to our next stop, Kings Church in the city centre, where I was lined up to meet the legendary 'heavyfoot' Andy Hawthorne, internationally renowned for his pioneering music production with The World Wide Message Tribe, and one of the most well-known Christians in England. His pure-bred Mancunian image, hard-line preaching and insatiable desire to see Manchester's toughest young people hearing and responding to Jesus were enough of a reputation to send me running for cover. The few minutes we spent with Andy that day did nothing to allay my fears over my future; having heard that I had been offered the job as team leader and would be moving to Openshaw to start this new project, Andy looked at me, perhaps the most inappropriately dressed urban missionary he'd seen in a while, and said more or less these exact words. 'Well ... you will have your house burgled. You will have your car stolen. You will be assaulted and abused by the people you try to serve. But if you still want to come to Manchester, then come.' Talk about the hard sell! Later I would appreciate Andy's brutal honesty, but at the time it really didn't make me want to buy in.

Six months later, after an exhausting wrestle with God, my conscience and anyone else who cared to contribute, I was on my way up the M6 to move into a house in the heart of the Toxteth Street estate, probably the darkest part of this dark community. I didn't sleep for one minute during the first night in that house. Every slight noise had me jumping out of bed to check that I wasn't being burgled or having my car stolen, and I could hear cars being driven at high speeds all around, and people shouting up and down the street. I was scared.

Andy was right to give me the worst-case scenario on my interview day, but what I found as I lived in Openshaw for a few weeks and months is that there was a lot of joy here too. People were friendly, the sun still shone, snow still lay thick on the ground in winter, you could hear laughter in the streets and most of what I considered to be threatening noise was just people communicating. After a while it actually began to feel like home.

After six years in Openshaw, Hannah and I turned a somewhat unexpected corner in our ministry. Once we surfaced from the first few months of parenthood and actually began to function as relatively normal adults again, we realised that more than ever before we were in need of our community. Whereas before we had always been service providers, running youth clubs and toddler groups, special events and activities, we were suddenly in need of the support and services that our community provides. Naturally since our children were born we have spent a whole lot more time at the doctor's surgery, the toddler group, the library, the nursery and the park than we ever have before, but the key difference has been that as beneficiaries of the services we line up like everyone else and gratefully accept what is on offer.

When we begin to do things with the community it opens up a level of relationship with local people that is difficult to achieve when you only do things for the community. As we have opened ourselves up to be helped we have found that all kinds of new opportunities have arisen for us to serve our friends and neighbours.

Another noticeable change occurred when we handed over the leadership of Openshaw Community Church and the Eden Project to Sam and Nicci in February 2007: it was as if, in giving up our 'role' and 'title', we suddenly became a little more equal with our neighbours, a little more anonymous and a little more approachable. As well as people's changing perceptions we have found that we are now able to be more committed to the things that our neighbours are creating like residents groups, home watch services, community companies and special events, all of which give us a deeper connection with our people than we previously encountered.

This is true in many different ways when you live in a deprived community. When our neighbours get upset about youth nuisance and car crime and they call a meeting with the police and local councillors about how to tackle it, our church can have a credible and valuable role in that meeting because we are genuinely concerned that all our people are affected by such issues. When the regeneration planners informed our community that they were going to knock all the houses down, many people were deeply upset at the prospect of losing their family home, while others were delighted at the thought of new modern housing replacing the tired terraces.

Our congregation were similarly divided on the issue, but we were able to have a very real understanding of the issues and as residents have a strong voice to the regeneration partners to ensure that each individual case was treated justly and that no-one was displaced unnecessarily. Our influential role in the renewal of Openshaw has not come about because we have a church building there, but because we are all local residents who understand the needs of the community.

Something that has surprised me as I've read and re-read General Booth's book is that he consistently uses language that separates himself from the people who he so desperately wanted to serve. He was clearly a man who was deeply passionate about doing everything he could to eradicate poverty, but the notion of becoming poor himself in order to do so was evidently outside of his sphere of vision. He is particularly concerned about rich and poor children being educated together: 'The common school to which the children of thieves, harlots and drunkards are driven, to sit side by side with our little ones, is often by no means a temple of all the virtues ... The bad infect the good, and your boy and girl come back reeking with the contamination of bad associates, and familiar with the coarsest obscenity of the slums.'[5]

This is, of course, one of the real dangers of living in deprived communities. Inevitably we get affected, and our children do too. I have managed to live a full 35 years without ever being involved in a serious fight, but unfortunately a few weeks ago my son took his first right hook from a boy twice his age when they were fighting over an ironing board at the toddler group. As I comforted Joel and dried the tears from his bruised face I sensed something of Booth's concern: how will my kids turn out, and what if they get hurt? What if they get bullied? What if they get swept along with a bad crowd and end up on ASBOs? But I remain convinced that the best way to impact other families is to live our lives alongside them showing respect, sharing the struggle and learning together.

CHURCH?

If we are to successfully make our journey back into Darkest England and begin to build new worshipping communities there, we are going to have to rediscover what it really means to be the church. We cannot rely on old models – either those that worked for Booth 100 years ago or those which bear fruit among the middle and upper classes of society today. I have no intention of offering you any such model for how church should look in Darkest England, except for the broad brush strokes offered by the chapter titles of this book and to say that each worshipping community should reflect the culture of its own environment. We should not be surprised if one congregation functions entirely differently to another – in fact, this should be something to celebrate. Our job is not the import, export or preservation of culture, it is to continue the ministry which Jesus started by announcing the good news of the Kingdom, which he ultimately did by planting the seed and watching it grow. The seed of the Kingdom will inevitably grow differently in Darkest England but we will have to learn not to fear things that may look unfamiliar.

The term 'church' originates from the Greek word *ekklesia* which is a word used in Greek secular culture to mean 'those who have been summoned together'. Originally the word had no particular religious meaning, in fact it was often used to describe an angry mob of troublemakers until the term was adopted by the first Christians.

They used it to refer to 'those who have been summoned together by God'. As the early church used the word as a description of themselves, the word '*ekklesia*' evolved to hold the enhanced, theocentric meaning we use today, declaring God to be the cause of this gathering.

According to Hans Kung, the term *ekklesia* evolved to hold three very important, complementary characteristics which remain foundational to our understanding of what the church is.

Ekklesia: Congregation – the continual coming together of people in a regular event or meeting.

Ekklesia: Community – the constant, local group or community which is initially forged by the regular meeting together but exists outside of any structured meeting or planned schedule. This is enhanced by shared vision and values and fuelled in deep-spirited friendships.

***Ekklesia*: The Church** – the belief that each local church, however small, represents the fullness of The Worldwide Church of God and in one sense part of the body of Christ but is also complete in and of itself.

These, says Kung, complement each other and should be seen as interconnected ways of understanding the multifaceted *ekklesia*.[7] This kind of insight into the meaning of church is helpful as we reflect on what it means to be the church in Darkest England today. David Watson, in his book *I Believe in the Church*, refers to the community aspect of *ekklesia* and comments that 'each local church must learn to live as true community seven days a week'.[7] He goes on to say that relationships in church communities must be more than a superficial connection for an hour or two on Sunday – there must be a depth of giving and understanding from one to another.

One of the most striking passages of scripture regarding this broader understanding of church is Acts 2:42–47 where a description is given of the life of the first Christians: learning, sharing, eating, meeting, praying, signs and wonders, growth – true community. The whole paragraph conjures up a dynamic image of community living, which for most of the western church now is nothing more than a dream or an ideal. On reflection we might ask, 'Would a short description of our twenty-first-century church be anything like as exciting?'

Within a few months of living in Openshaw there were six other people from our team living on my street. The closest was just three doors away but there are only 120 houses on the street so we were all close. Similar numbers lived on the immediately surrounding streets, about 20 in all. Every day people would call round, always to chat, often to pray and to eat, and many hours were spent late into the night making plans for our great mission endeavours. Even after a long night of youth work we would inevitably end up debriefing over a brew and some toast in someone's front room. Late night callouts when trouble kicked off, water fights in the street and whole nights spent making the most of freshly fallen snow – in such times we met with God and deep-spirited friendships were formed, the ones that the church should be made of and the type in which spiritual giants are grown. Of course this kind of living is not without sacrifice – there is a lack of any privacy, everything is everyone's business, people know what time you sleep and what time you rise, where you shop and how much you spend, but this only helped us to live open, transparent lives which make accountability and holiness a 24/7 thing.

The tragedy is that our experience of church life is by no means the norm. For many of us *ekklesia* has become nothing more than a series of meetings and programmes that we attend. Those meetings may be many and varied, they may be inspirational, spirit-filled and meaningful but if they are all we have then we are missing out on so much of what church community has to offer. Building churches which can facilitate genuine community outside of a formal setting without devaluing the congregational aspect is a key part of our move into Darkest England, as is creating places where people and relationships take priority over programmes and meetings.

The church should be a community that is meeting together constantly, at various times sharing meals, going for a run, helping with the kids and picking up shopping. We must learn again how to give generously of our time, to let our brothers and sisters see us at our worst as well as our best, when we are coping and when we are not.

In 1 Thessalonians 2:8 Paul says, '. . . we were delighted to share with you not only the gospel of God but our lives as well . . .'.

This will remain a pipe dream if we live miles from our church communities. I suspect that Paul was referring to something more than attending two meetings on Sundays and a cell group in the week when he wrote this; we cannot expect to effectively share our lives with people by commuting to and from our churches.

The argument may come, 'But there are no churches in my neighbourhood which I could go to',[8] or 'There are actually no churches in my neighbourhood at all'. I have two friends, one in the UK and one in the USA, who faced such dilemmas in their different contexts. Wanting to remain true to the ideal of *ekklesia* and incarnational living, they gathered up a group of friends and moved into tough communities to be church together. They have no buildings or programmes and no intention of getting any, they simply meet in each other's homes, praying, learning and breaking bread, and then they serve the community in all kinds of practical ways, demonstrating and communicating the Gospel through their lives and their words. They function, broadly speaking, under the umbrella of larger denominations but they are essentially independent bodies of believers experiencing *ekklesia* in its fullness and sharing their lives with each other and with their local community. It can be done.

PLANTING STRATEGY MUST BE FOCUSED ON POOR COMMUNITIES

The 10 DAWN[9] principles for responsible church planting provide the church with a framework for how different groups should go about initiating work in a new area so as not to cause offence to others and to maximise resources. These are all well and good but they say little about where such planting should take place, apart from giving priority to areas where there is 'no resident gospel witness or church'. At first read this makes perfect sense but the reality is that much of the church's planting strategy in recent years has been based around suburban communities. It is not my intention to denigrate any of the work that has taken place in those areas but I do want to take issue with the avoidance of planting in poorer communities where I believe the need is greater.

I cannot say that there is no need for churches to be planted in wealthier communities – however, where there is wealth there is usually mobility, whether that be personal transport, access to public transport or generous friends who can provide lifts. There is also communication: telephones, mobile phones, email and the Internet, which all aid relationship building and community. Generally speaking, people from wealthier neighbourhoods are better educated, have better social skills and are likely to travel frequently to places outside of their immediate environment for any number of reasons. It is not unreasonable then to suppose that such people could, if it were really necessary, make a short journey to involve themselves in the life of a church.

Such mobility and communication is to most of us the norm, and for some it might even be a basic requisite for life, but not so in Darkest England. The inner city is very territorial and it is common for people young and old to never leave the confines of their small patch. The kids who grow up on the streets of the Toxteth Street estate would not expect to venture outside of their terraces, which are no more than a quarter of a square mile in total. Many times when we have taken groups of young people on the half-hour drive to the Peak District, they have been amazed at how far you can go; last summer we took a group to Southport Beach and many of them sat staring at the sea, which they had never seen before. In order to travel you need many things: firstly, you need a reason to go somewhere like work or friends or shopping, and most people in Darkest England do not have any of these.

If they did have a reason to travel somewhere they would need money. Getting the bus is expensive, so it would need to be something really important like a hospital appointment to spend

£3 of their food money. You also need self-esteem to give you the confidence to walk in to a new place and be sure that you could cope if anything went wrong, and a degree of intelligence and literacy to understand the transport system. You need to make sure you look right; any of us who have been to new places know how we make sure we are dressed appropriately so that we don't stand out or look silly. To someone without any of these things, the world outside their immediate locality can seem a very daunting place. I recently met a lady who has lived in Manchester for all of her 33 years and she has never been to the city centre, which is about a 15-minute bus ride away from her house. So, unlike the wealthier classes, the underclass stay at home in the paradoxical safety of the most dangerous communities in Britain.

When we begin to understand these mobility issues we will see that our priority must be to establish our churches in these communities with groups of Christians living, worshipping and serving in the streets and houses around about so that the poor don't once again feel marginalised and excluded from our opulent megachurches with their car park attendants and coffee house interiors. The poor will not make the geographical or cultural journeys to those establishments but the rich might.

'In spite of the noble affirmations of Christianity, the church has often lagged behind in its concern for social justice and too often has been content to mouth pious irrelevances and sanctimonious trivialities.'[10]

Martin Luther King

References and Notes

1. Booth, p. 216.
2. Booth, p. 138.
3. Lloyd, M., *Café Theology* (Alpha International, 2006), p. 131.
4. Gunten in Ward, P., *Liquid Church* (Paternoster Press, 2002), p. 54.
5. Booth, p. 69.
6. Kung, H., *The Church* (Search Press, 1971), pp. 79–87.
7. Watson, D., *I Believe in the Church* (Hodder & Stoughton, 1993), p. 71.
8. Such an argument does rather reveal just how much the consumer culture mentioned in Chapter 2 has infected even our perspective of the body of Christ. But I don't intend to go into that here.
9. DAWN aims at mobilising the whole body of Christ in whole countries in a determined effort to complete the great commission by working towards the goal of providing an Evangelical congregation for every village and neighbourhood of every class, kind and condition of people in the whole country. Montgomery, J., *DAWN 2000* (Highland, 1989).
10. King, M. L., *Strength To Love* (Fortress Press, 1981).

4

TRANSFORMATIONAL EXPERIENCES

When I first heard about Tony's debt to the loan shark I told him I wanted to meet the oppressor who had kept him and his two boys literally scavenging for food for five months. His response was swift and stern: 'You better not tell him I've told you, he'll send the gypsies round with bats to beat the kids if he ever finds out that you know. He must never find out that I've told you.' The fear in the eyes of this tough Manchester man who stood a full six inches taller than me suggested that knocking on the shark's door to ask for his benefit book back might not be the best idea I'd had that day, but I knew that doing nothing was not an option here. If I had moved 300 miles to Manchester for anything, it was to stand up for people who are getting bullied and beaten, and this was certainly one such occasion.

We hatched a plan. On Wednesday morning I would go to the post office with Tony. I would hide out of sight of 'Moysie' (the loan shark) and we would take enough money to pay off the debt in full – this would cost his whole week's benefit plus forty pounds, and we would take another twenty pounds so that there would be no need to borrow any more money for that week. When the money was handed over Tony would get his benefit book back and he would be set free from the oppressor. Tony said that if anyone saw me he would say that I was his brother who'd come to help him out. It's not our policy to encourage lying so I told him to tell the truth if anyone spotted me.

Wednesday came and the church gathered to pray early in the morning as I went to the cashpoint to withdraw the cash. My hand was literally shaking as I snatched the bunch of ten pound notes from the machine. Tony and Justin climbed into the back of my car and crouched down behind the seats. Tony was still insistent that he would protect me by saying that I was his brother, while I still protested that he should tell the truth. We parked and Tony got out of the car about a hundred yards from the post office and I watched him walk off down the road in my mirror, scrounging a cig from an acquaintance. Meanwhile a huge silver BMW pulled up right behind my car, and in the driving seat was a huge man covered in tattoos and wearing a gold chain which looked thick enough to hold up a suspension bridge. In the passenger seat was a 15-year-old boy who I knew really well from our youth clubs; perhaps more importantly, he knew me.

Some fairly large pennies started to drop in my brain as I pieced together a picture of who this man was and where his teenaged accomplice fitted in. I realised that he was the son of Moysie, already a championship boxer and being groomed as a heavy for the family business. As all this was spinning around in my head, Justin, who was still crouched in the back seat, popped his head up to see what was happening and in doing so he blew our cover – Moysie Senior and Junior spotted him, and me, as I tried my best to conceal him from view. Now they knew that I was there with Tony and they also knew that I was from the church and not Tony's brother. I figured we were in a whole heap of trouble that could easily be made worse by Tony lying to cover my identity. All we could do was pray that he told the truth and hope that somehow the truth would set us free.

A few minutes passed and Tony strolled out of the post office. There was a quick exchange with the henchman and he wandered away from the car to the far end of the street. The BMW pulled into the road and spun round with a screech just in front of us, smoke rising from the burning tyres and the car pulled up slowly alongside our Fiat until the two drivers' doors were nearly touching. I hardly dared look but forced an emotionless glance at the oppressor. His face said – 'I've clocked you, you had better watch your back.' He sped off, and when the smoke had cleared we drove off down the road and Tony climbed back in. 'That's strange,' he said. 'He asked me who was sitting in the car and I meant to say that you were my brother but what came out was – "He's from the church."' The rest of the journey home no-one really said anything – Tony kissed and caressed his benefit book as if it were a fair maiden and Justin just laughed and giggled at the thought of food from the shop instead of the skip. I was left to reflect upon the maths of it all: three lives utterly transformed for sixty quid and some courage.

TRANSFORMATION PEOPLE

What does it mean to be transformation people in the heart of Darkest England, where need is all around and comes in many different guises? Jesus seems to have perceived transformation in the broadest terms, and when he came into contact with people their lives and often their circumstances were different as a result. A notable example of this would be Zacchaeus, who turned from his life of greed and selfishness in Luke 19 to become a man identified by generosity and justice. The woman who was saved from being stoned in John 8 could never have expected the gracious response Jesus offered her, which with a single sentence transformed her life expectancy from a few torturous minutes to potentially long and happy years. The centurion who mourned his beloved slave but returned from Jesus to find him fit and well in Luke 7 went from grief to celebration at the hand of Jesus. When Jesus fed the 5,000 in Mark 6 he provided a transformational experience for them, as he did at the wedding in John 2 when he turned water into wine. Quenching the thirst of the 30 and filling the stomachs of the hungry is a transformational act. Contact with Jesus and his kingdom always brings about transformation, and contact with the church, his body, should be no different.

Ephesians 1:7–10 describes for us the full transformation that comes with the knowledge of God through Christ, and it is only through Christ that full transformation can occur as a person has not just their outward appearance transformed but their inward character. Typically pragmatic, Booth says: 'Hence, unless you change their character your labour will be lost. You may clothe the drunkard, fill his purse with gold, establish him in a well-furnished home and in three or six or twelve months he will once more be on the embankment.' We should then also be actively looking for the miraculous: praying for the sick, living by faith, being agents of grace and salvation in our communities, always ready to share the life-transforming gospel with neighbours and those who we come into contact with.

However, that does not mean to say that transformation is only a spiritual matter; on the contrary, transformation should be occurring in and around our daily lives through our generosity, our positive attitude, the deep-spirited joy and our love as well as through the regenerating work of the Holy Spirit.

WHY WE DO WHAT WE DO

People are often cynical about the church, and one of the main reasons for their concern is they wonder about our motives for doing what we do. They are worried about proselytisation, evangelism, making converts – none of which are very politically correct things to do in twenty-first-century Britain. I observe these concerns in multi-agency partnerships, schools, neighbourhood renewal groups, parents of young people and many other parts of society that we come into contact with, and perhaps their concerns are valid. As a parent I don't want just anyone influencing my children, I want to know exactly what values and beliefs are being peddled before I will let them attend a group or club. I want to know up front what motives people have to do what they do and I see that as a responsible attitude to have whether we are talking about parents, schools or multi-agency partnerships.

It seems that the more people have shied away from spiritual influence, the more some parts of the church have insisted that evangelism and gaining converts is our primary focus. Whilst I agree that there should always be freedom for us to share our personal faith and the opportunity to encourage people to discover Christ in their own journey of faith, we must be careful not to be so dogmatic that we believe everything to be worthless if it doesn't result in conversion. If all of our works are only valuable if they result in conversion then we have wasted a whole lot of time over the last 2,000 years. If all our kind and loving actions in society are just bait to get people to the altar on Sunday, then they are not really kind and loving actions, but loaded with hidden agendas, and we should not be surprised if people are suspicious.

Some Christians might argue that we are just getting people interested and then when they've warmed to us we give them the real blessing of freedom and salvation, but I would argue that we shouldn't need to hide the good news behind anything. The parables of the treasure hidden in a field and the pearl in Matthew 13 both presume that the kingdom of heaven is exactly what the world is looking for, those who are searching and those who are not, so there should be no need to use good works to attract people to the kingdom.

We do good works not because they are bait for the convert, but because they transform lives and because the scriptures command us to. In the very beginning of the Bible, Genesis 1, mankind is given dominion over all the earth, to care for the birds of the air, the beasts of the field and the fish of the sea. Humanity was in a perfect relationship with creation, with each other and with God; that's where the Bible starts, with our humanity and our role in creation. Our mission is to care for God's beloved creation and to maintain and restore those relationships to their former glory where they have been broken. Too much of our activity begins with Genesis 3 – the Fall, the sin, the separation from God – and never touches the other aspects of what mission really is.

The kind of transformation we must seek is a holistic transformation which restores dignity to those who have been disgraced, which offers prospects to those who've been excluded, which offers freedom to those held captive, and which offers hospitality to the hungry and the homeless. Helping people to restore their relationship with God is part of our mission but it isn't the alpha and the omega.

There is a sense in which all of our actions, not just those that result in conversion, are part of the redemptive process which God has set in place. 1 Corinthians 15:58 says, 'your labour ... is not in vain.' Mother Theresa of Calcutta echoed this when she said, 'Nothing done in love will be lost' – that means our care of the planet, our caring for people, helping them to order their lives, helping people to reconnect with God, each other and creation, bringing about justice and caring for the poor are all valuable in themselves and not only, as we sometimes believe, if they result in a person joining our church.

In his book *Café Theology*, Michael Lloyd suggests that all the efforts and good works that we offer in our life time will, in the end times, be somehow gathered up and used as part of the creation of the new heaven and the new earth. He says, 'We don't bring about the resurrection: God does. But when He does, all that we are and all that we have done that is not incompatible with the Kingdom of God will be there, shot through with love and the glory of God.'[1] What an amazing thought.

SIMPLE TRANSFORMATION

I started this chapter with perhaps the most dramatic transformation encounter that I have had but the truth is that for most of the time transformation happens in the smallest actions of our daily lives – this is especially true when we have relocated ourselves into places of great need. A lady knocked on my friends' door last week. We have met the lady before, she clearly has some mental health problems and she was crying and talking about killing herself. We are not sure what had gone wrong, perhaps her medication had got mixed up and sent her into a depression. After half an hour and a hot cup of tea in the warmth of their home they had managed to calm her down and she said 'I think I'd like to go home now.' So they drove the lady home, stopping on the way to get some credit for her gas card and some food, offered a prayer and left her settled, warm and fed. Transformation occurred out of willingness to do some simple things. And it gets simpler. One hot Sunday afternoon a group of us got playing with some local children and water pistols in the street. What started out as a few squirts between friends soon escalated into delirium in the street: 40 people of all ages, parents, kids, teenagers, adults like me who should know better ... racing around the street using anything we could to throw water over each other. Good, clean, soaking wet fun! I noticed a man sat in his window watching for an hour or more.

When we all finally collapsed with exhaustion I went to the man's door to check that he wasn't cross about the disturbance in the street, but what I found was the opposite – he was absolutely thrilled to have enjoyed watching everyone having such fun. 'I've not seen anything like this around here for years,' he said. 'I was on my way to the betting shop, but this was much better.' Transformation occurred out of a water fight.

And simpler still. When our friend Lizzie was on the bus one day, an Iranian man sat next to her and she said 'Good morning'. They had a polite but limited conversation across a very difficult language barrier, and not really knowing what else to do she wrote the name, address and phone number of our church on a scrap of paper and handed it to him as she got off the bus. The result was that Akbah, a lonely asylum-seeker who had been smuggled into Britain in the back of a truck, became part of our community, regularly worshipping with us, attending a small group and even travelling with me to be involved in some training with the Salvation Army. Transformation came out of saying 'Good morning'.

HUNGER FOR TRANSFORMATION

Our world is looking for transformation. Our local free paper carries a large advert every single week which says on it 'Transform', advertising all kinds of ways to enhance your appearance through cosmetic surgery. People are constantly searching for the perfect image, if not under the surgeon's knife then by buying the right car, having the right hobby or the right haircut.

People believe that money might be the key to transformation, and have a national obsession with playing the lottery which offers false hope of untold riches to millions of people every week. Many of the poorest players believe that this is their only hope of escaping their circumstances.

It could also be argued that there is a heightened desire for spiritual encounters as an ever-increasing number of people are looking to mediums and psychics for some sort of spiritual revelation. Many of the box office hits of the last decade have had overtly spiritual themes, while entertainers like Derek Acorah appear with greater frequency on regular daytime TV and consistently pack out venues in our towns and cities with their 'spiritual' shows. People all around are craving transformation and many of them expect that the transformation they need is outside of the physical realm.

In this climate of spiritual searching the sad fact is that for most people their local church is the last place they would look for a spiritual or transformational experience, and most people do not associate churches with either of these things. Perhaps our routines and rituals have become devoid of any meaning, or perhaps they just lack power to instigate real change in our contemporary culture. In order to be transformation people we need to ensure that whenever people encounter our church, whether that is meeting one of our members at work or walking into a meeting on Sunday morning, they find real, gritty, life-transforming spirituality which is not overacted by pious talk or religious jargon but demonstrated in real, ordinary lives touched by the living God. People will respond best to our own experience and journey of faith. To acknowledge that we are not the finished article but are intentionally discovering what it means to be a Christian is not a statement of weakness but an honest statement about our condition. 2 Corinthians 3:18 says 'And we, who with unveiled faces all reflect the Lord's glory, are being transformed into his likeness'. Our transformation is an ongoing process and people are more likely to be interested by church communities that acknowledge the journey that they are on than by people who claim to have it all sewn up already.

RESPECT AGENDA

Once we have committed ourselves to holistic transformation mission, which includes evangelism but is not defined by it, we must work out how to achieve our mission in Darkest England. Everything we do must offer to our community hope, love, reconciliation and advocacy without ever becoming patronising – people may be struggling to make their lives work properly without help, they may be poor, addicted or uneducated but they deserve to be treated with dignity and respect. Most people do not need reminding of the mess they are in. From time to time during my years in the inner city I have experienced wealthy, educated Christians who thought it was their right to drive into the neighbourhood and preach the Gospel through a megaphone (usually this amounted to telling people that they are sinners: a fact which most are only too acutely aware of), then climb into their cars and drive off. Others have stuffed tracts containing the same message, 'you are a sinner', through people's doors. Frankly I find this offensive and I know my neighbours do too. In fact the street corner preacher and the tract lady are the kind of 'missionaries' that make people retreat further and further from the church.

I find this kind of ministry so offensive because we wouldn't do it to our non-Christian friends. I have been a Christian for about 18 years and in that time I have sat in countless small groups and committee meetings where we have discussed at length how to communicate our faith with our friends or work colleagues. The ideas that arose out of those meetings have been many and varied, from great costly events to intimate dinner parties, courses, barbeques and even holidays, but in all those meetings I don't think I have once heard the suggestion that we should find a public place, catch our friends by surprise and then with a megaphone tell them they are a sinner and damned to hell.

Neither have I heard anyone propose buying up the stock of tracts at the local Christian bookshop and pushing them through the doors of all our friends and business associates. I'm glad I have not heard these suggestions in such meetings because they would be monstrously disrespectful to the people concerned, not to mention to the Gospel itself. We generally don't think that this is an acceptable way to communicate important matters with people who we respect. Why, then, do people presume that it is OK to treat 'poor' or 'uneducated' people in this way? There can only be one answer and it is that as wealthy, educated successful people we sometimes presume that we have the right to flex our social, intellectual and religious muscles in front of the poor and they will somehow come flocking to us.

I have a rule which I apply to all my ministry, my worship, my preaching and my evangelism, which is that I always ask myself: 'If my football mates were here now, would I behave in the same way and say the same things?' In other words: would I do what I am doing to people that I admire? Perhaps your benchmark should be your non-Christian boss or a family member but whoever it is make sure that if you are seeking holistic transformation among the poor, you don't do anything that you wouldn't do to someone who you respect.

UNEXPECTED TRANSFORMATION

When you realise what transformation involves, you quickly realise that getting involved in people's messy lives is costly. Many times I've been warned by well-meaning friends not to get involved in people's lives, not to interfere. I've also been lectured by professionals in the world of social care about 'maintaining a professional distance from the clientele'. While I can understand and appreciate such concern for our well-being, I can't help thinking how glad I am that Jesus didn't keep such rules and boundaries with those he met, and that leads me directly to the conclusion that for the Christian who is genuinely seeking transformation there can be no such boundaries.

On the wall by my desk is a picture of Kim and Ann. It reminds me to pray for a mother and daughter who I have not seen for about two years. When we first met Kim she was on a Methadone[2] programme but continued to use heroin on a regular basis. Hannah and I involved ourselves with Kim and over a long period of time we got to know her very well. She was frequently around our house and we regularly went to her house. She got involved in our church and became a very well-known character in our congregation as she regularly interrupted the preacher on a Sunday morning to ask for some clarification on a particular point. There were times when Kim would pray the most amazing prayers, say the most profound things; I clearly remember one Sunday morning when she came into church and asked if we could go into the back room to pray so Hannah, Lizzie and I accompanied her and we gathered round her as she knelt on the floor crying and uttering great prayers of repentance which moved us all to tears. Kim could be the most loving, sincere, sweet person sometimes and I always believed that she wanted to find a better path for herself but drugs had got a hold on her that seemed to be unshakeable.

Much as we came to love her, our friendship with Kim was a costly one. Many times we were let down and disappointed as she seemed unable to keep to the decisions that she made. She stole from us on a number of occasions and she stole from our friends; she borrowed things and never returned them, she told lies even when she didn't need to. To some extent we expected our good will to be abused and we expected to get hurt but we never expected that we would both have our hearts broken by the love we had for her.

Kim would come for tea at our house at least once each week and on one such occasion, between mouthfuls of food, she casually announced to us that she was pregnant. We were horrified, knowing the chaos that surrounded her life, the systematic abuse of drugs and the many unsavoury characters which played bit parts in her life we could think of at least a hundred good reasons why bringing a child into the equation was a bad idea. However we supported her throughout the pregnancy and on 4 September 2002 beautiful Ann was born at just 5 pounds[3] and placed straight on the special care baby unit to be nursed through withdrawal. Two weeks later we collected mother and baby from the hospital and delivered them safely home. The next year had its ups and downs but Kim and Ann both coped reasonably well with lots of help from the church and the health services. On Ann's first birthday I dedicated her in our morning meeting and we had a party afterwards.

It wasn't long after that that things started to go bad. The drugs were becoming more and more part of Kim's life again and we would regularly see her out late at night with Ann in tow, knocking at the dealers' doors and getting into trouble, and we feared she had gone back to crime and vice to pay for her habit. For the sake of Ann's safety we took the tough decision to inform social services of our concerns and, despite our plea to the social worker to maintain our anonymity, she divulged our identity to Kim. The response was frightening as Kim came to the church and verbally went for Hannah, she vandalised our car twice and would stand outside our house late at night shouting threats at the window. The head of social services, who came personally to apologise to us, advised us to move out of the area for our own safety; of course this was never an option for us but from this point on, although we tried on many occasions to rebuild things, our relationship never recovered.

A few weeks after things had died down I saw Kim with Ann just down the street from the church, and as I approached I was longing for her to look up and speak to me – longing for her to forget what had happened recently and remember the many happy times, the trips to the beach and walks in the park. My heart was racing with hopeful anticipation as I got closer, then she looked up, saw me coming and quickly looked away. She turned her back on me, refusing to give me eye contact, and ushered Ann away down a side street. I felt like a bit of my heart scurried off after them.

And as I wept during the rest of my walk down the street, something dawned on me. I came to Openshaw full of dreams and ideas about transforming the community and thought long and hard about how my work here would impact the local people and change things for the better, and to some degree I have seen some of the change that I had hoped to experience. However, what I began to realise that day was that in many cases the transformation that has taken place has been far more inside me than inside the different characters that I have come into contact with: Kim went back to her life as if she had never met us, but we will never go back to the way our life was before we met her.

Kim and many others like her who have come into our lives for various reasons have left an indelible mark on us through the things they have taught us and the way they have accepted us into their worlds. I know that our lives will never be the same since the day we met Kim. We have learned how rich we are to have friends and family who care about us, and how fortunate we are to have never experienced the horrors of addiction, which drains you of dignity if not life itself. We have developed a sense of responsibility in the way we live, seeking to be generous with our time, our home and our belongings, not living extravagant lives while others suffer, realising that the decisions that we make about our lives affect the chances of others. We know that we can make choices which offer transformational experiences for others who would otherwise be trapped in an endless cycle of poverty, addiction, abuse or some other social ill.

We have come to respect people from all kinds of background with all kinds of problems, to see people that have different lives to us as equals who have rich and colourful lives themselves, whose stories reveal a lifetime of fascinating experiences. They are not there to be lectured and bullied by the rich and the educated, but are there to be loved and befriended, and as we allow ourselves to get close enough to be affected we will undoubtedly encounter for ourselves a transformational experience as we meet God right there among the poor.

Our life in Darkest England will be one that expects to see transformation occurring all around us every day, in the ordinary and in the extraordinary. When we give everything we have to see people's lives transformed in practical ways and rely on God to facilitate the ultimate regenerating transformation of the 'sinner to saint' then we will be in a very fertile place indeed. But beware, no-one should set foot on the path to Darkest England if they themselves are not prepared to be transformed by what they will find there. The personal growth and transformation that will take place in any person embarking on this mission to Darkest England is something to be expected, facilitated and celebrated.

> 'Only through love transformation of the so-called wicked ones is possible.'
>
> **Sri Sathya Baba (Indian Spiritual Leader, 1926)**

References and Notes

1. Lloyd, M., *Café Theology* (Alpha International, 2006), p. 227.
2. Methadone is a heroin substitute which is often prescribed to drug users. For some reason the authorities believe it to be less addictive than heroin but those who we know who have tried to kick it would tell you different.
3. Heroin users generally have small babies which are often premature, and according to many, unnaturally easy labours. Many babies born to heroin users are born addicted to heroin and need to be weaned off in their first few weeks of life.

5

I have dedicated a whole chapter of this book to the issue of addiction because, as we have discovered and as you have realised from the stories you have read throughout earlier chapters, addiction is cast in a starring role in Darkest England. It is, in our experience, a devastating and widespread social cancer that has affected and infected so many of the people who make up our community; if people aren't addicts themselves, then they most likely have a family member or friend who is.

According to research by the Church Urban Fund, around 3.5 million people in Britain used drugs in the last year, and 8.2 million people have an alcohol disorder.[1]

The children of substance-misusing parents are often hit the hardest: according to the Government Advisory Council on the Misuse of Drugs, 350,000 children are estimated to be at risk from parental and carer drug abuse in the UK, while 920,000 are living with parental alcohol misuse. More disturbing than these figures is the fact that children who live in homes where adults use drugs are seven times more likely to become drug users themselves.[2] The cycle is vicious and tough to break.

With the appearance of freedom, many drug users walk the streets of Openshaw daily, frequenting the phone boxes, the chemist and the drug dens, but in reality freedom is not a word that they have any concept of. They may not have been incarcerated in Her Majesty's Prison yet, but they carry their cell everywhere they go, unable to break free from the demon that drives their every move.

They are in every sense captive: bound by the chains of physical and psychological addiction. Some would argue that a life of drug dependency is the worst detention of all. Not all addicts are drug users; many are alcoholics, a more upmarket vice in the strange social hierarchy of the underclasses. Alcoholism and drunkenness are deemed acceptable in Darkest England, despite their devastating effects on the human body and mind and the terrible impact that they have on family life, especially the children who miss out on so much when Mum or Dad is a heavy drinker.

I am all too aware that there are many people more qualified to speak on this subject than me. One alcoholic friend said to me recently, 'When I first met you five years ago you were totally naïve, but you're getting better and in about ten years' time, if you work hard, you might be OK at it.' If I wasn't aware of my shortcomings before, then I really am now! My purpose in writing is not to lecture on the best ways to treat alcoholism or drug addiction – if you're looking for such advice, there are plenty of resources available. My purpose is to open up a window into a world which exists largely outside the view and experience of the church and of the middle and upper classes. If we are serious about returning to Darkest England, then we will encounter people who are struggling with addiction. The audience before whom we will live out our Christianity will in many ways be captive and so we should begin to prepare our hearts and minds for what will undoubtedly be a costly, exciting and heart-breaking journey.

I have chosen to use the words of a person who knows what it is like to live a life of captivity through alcoholism. Tommy has been a close friend of ours for the last eight years, since he moved into the house next door. He is very much part of our church community and social group and he sometimes volunteers at our community activities. He was recently reunited with his daughter, who he had not seen for six years. Tommy is a character; a 'forty-something' Irishman with a story for every occasion, he'll tell you he's been the landlord of virtually every pub in London, and anywhere you've been – he's been there before you. I am grateful to him for allowing me to record and write this conversation as a transcript and for the typical honesty with which he speaks. Like most addicts and alcoholics, Tommy's life is full of ups and downs, and all we can say at this time is that the 'ups' are slowly becoming more frequent and the 'downs' less desperate. At the time of this conversation he was in a down time; after a long dry period he had been back on the drink for six months. His body was not actually able to hold any food or drink except alcohol and he had been this way for several weeks; he had had no gas or electricity in his house for five days and he had not slept more than two hours at a time for the same period. Christmas was five days away and there wasn't a single decoration in his house, no food and certainly no gift for his daughter, and he had no way of earning any money to rectify that situation. This is his story exactly as he told it, raw, unedited and fascinating:

Strangely enough most of my friends were drinking at a very young age but I'd seen my father who was bit of an "alco" but a great worker, and my mother who was a lovely lady and looked after us, but on the weekends would have a drink and they'd fight and that and I thought it wasn't for me. But I loved the bar and I loved entertaining people so I started working as a barman, but I didn't really have my first drink, I remember it was a pint of shandy, till I was about 16 or 17.

My mates who I loved dearly were having a couple of pints, not that it was for me, but it was a social thing – my peers were doing it and I wanted to fit in with them, I wanted to have a drink with lads and a chat and that, to be a man.

It was brilliant at the start. Then I came over and from earning £20 a week in Ireland I was in Kilburn and earning £75 a week, and that was a major improvement and beer was far much cheaper over here. You could get hammered on £10 and it was a great thing just to get hammered. And I was such a great barman and I had these ideas about myself and I wanted to impress people and all that, then it gradually became a situation where I would have lock-ins and just drink because I knew I could do it. But I absolutely didn't realise I was tearing it apart, that it would eventually cost me. It was just laughing, giggling, playing games, spending time with women, doing all the boys' things that you do, playing loads of pool till the early hours and gambling.

The worst of it has been my family. Splitting up with my woman, allowing my child to find himself in a situation where he obviously wasn't thinking straight and he got tragically killed. Missed my daughter for all the years, all of her life when I should have been there for her. I missed out on a lot of stuff and I've lost a lot of friends over the years, people I cared for and love, [even though] a lot of people stood by me.

Being part of a family, the infrastructure, being part of a family and growing up and spending Christmases and watching their birthdays and opening their presents, and family meals and friends around, and social evenings with your family and friends rather than with your so-called friends in the pub, because they are only so-called.

When you're drinking with these people they're your best mates but when you're not drinking with them they don't want to know you, and if you've got money in your pockets you'll find an absolute abundance of friends – people just want to be there especially if you've got a bit of a character about you and you can tell some jokes and get a giggle going. But when you find yourself on your arse and all that you haven't got a pot to piss in, nobody wants to know you. They're mercenary friends, if the money is good, like with mercenaries, you know they'll be there for you but once you've run out of cash they're not interested. I gave myself an illusion where I thought I was something special and I have this big big family of all these people, customers, and blokes and ladies that I drank with and I thought they'd always be with me forever, so I put my family to one side, whereas I should have put them first and then the other ones to one side. But in the long run, it's only from experience I've realised that was a big cock-up on my behalf. I think that I often give up the drink, every year now for the past few years I've given it an effort. Hopefully this year as from tomorrow I stop again and I like to think I could give it up for the whole year and maybe forever. I can't kid myself. I've found that when things are going good for myself I'm a happy chappy but when the shit hits the fan I don't know what to do and I find myself hiding in the bottom of a glass. I go for solace in the bottom of a bottle.

First thing in the morning when I wake up now I go straight to the bathroom, I'm really really ill. And I can't leave the house for the best part of half an hour and I can't, definitely not, look at food, a cup of tea or even a glass of water or orange juice, I'd throw it up. I get severe pains in my kidney and my groin and me back. My legs start feeling as if I'm carrying weights. And head pains, serious head pains, feel as though somebody has put some kind of major weight on top of my head because there's a lot of pressure on it. I get paranoid, sweats, I can't sleep unless I have alcohol. I haven't slept properly for months.

I won't cook, I won't tidy, I won't shave and I can't be bothered brushing my teeth, and the food thing, I maybe have three meals a week because I'm scared to eat and the only time I can eat is when I'm absolutely hammered. I have to be seriously pissed. So that means all day when I'm soberish I can't eat or I'll heave. Say about midnight when I'm absolutely hammered I'll eat a takeaway if I'm fortunate enough to have some money or I've begged it or I've borrowed. As I said yesterday I don't steal, but I've thought about it, when it's got that bad and I've thought 'God I need a drink' and nobody wants to help me and I need some money.

I've got some friends, not within the bar community, but in your community, the Christian community, and there I find I can spend loads of time with them when I'm not drinking, and I don't feel as though they're patronising me, I think that they do care. I enjoy their company and we can have giggles and laughs and I feel quite warm.

But as soon as I go for a drink and I do the stupid things, then my friends within the church, I avoid. I run away from them, which I'm quite ashamed of, because they did help me, to know I don't need a drink to be humorous, I'm quite funny at the best of times, and helpful. And that's annoying as well, I want to be helpful, I don't want to be a hindrance.

You [Gary[3]] moving away didn't help things but you've got a life to lead. Then Chris moved, and Chris was a big big pal to me. We used to talk about football, we used to watch videos, we'd go out, we'd spend time having a bite to eat, we'd go to the cinema, and didn't really feel like I needed these so-called friends in the pub, because it was just brilliant. I'd be with Chris one night, with Jon one night, it was just brilliant, I loved it. Then they moved away and that was a big loss to me.

The detox was brilliant. I was scared because I didn't know what was going to happen and you weren't allowed out for the first 72 hours. After the first day or two I stopped climbing the walls and had proper meals, and talking to other alcoholics about how much it created a major disaster in their lives, I thought yes, I can go back and I never even considered a drink, it was the last thing on my mind.

When I first connected with the church I had just packed the Crown pub in and got a house. I found myself living next door to you and Hannah. Because you're a good Christian you introduced yourself to me and invited me in for something to eat, which I miss now.

You didn't preach to me but I understood what you were trying to do, you were trying to help the community and trying to help all these youngsters, so I thought right, well I've explained to them that I don't believe in God and that I'm not really that interested. But as a person, and a good person I believe, I wanted to be helpful, so I said to you could I help in any way, and after a while I did my minibus training and helped out.

First of all when I first came to church I remember I was bricking it, I thought how am I going to handle this, everybody preaching and all that, but it wasn't like that. It didn't take the first couple of sessions, probably just the first fifteen or twenty minutes, and I felt quite comfortable. I met some brilliant people, just brilliant amazing people, and I just thought these are so beautiful and they've got something like God or the Holy Spirit or something like that but I haven't got a clue about that. But I thought it might be interesting to grab a hold.

For a while, when I was doing the Alpha sessions and when I was praying I'd go out of here feeling like twenty men. But usually it takes me a load of drink to feel like that, to feel unbeatable. But I found myself without any alcohol feeling amazing, but then I lost it. I can't believe how I felt at the time and how I want that back, because it was a good, good, feeling, and I had brilliant people around me. And I want to be involved in that again.

A friend should be a friend in all different types of times and should be there for you. But I found that when I was sober and I was involved coming to the church people were giving me a lot of time and interest and giving me phone calls and wanting to know if I wanted to go out and have a meal or go to the movies.

But since I hit the drink again, I don't know if it's me, but I've found that I've been left out and I've become angry. It's not that I need mollycoddling, you can't wrap me in cotton wool, I know that because I'm a grown up or I'm supposed to be, although I don't act it, but I need that TLC.

I really miss out on that, on the bites to eat. I feel as if I had a few more phone calls, it would make a big difference to myself. It would make me feel wanted. I think that's what it is with me, I do need to feel wanted. I think "where's the Christian side of you lot?" because I want you to want me, want to feel wanted. But I don't feel like that, I totally don't feel like that, I feel chucked to one side. Then when I become sober again I do get a lot of help, and you come and visit me, and try to help, and I'm involved. When I'm drinking nobody is interested.

I don't think I'm understood at all. I don't think you all understand alcoholism. I remember being very angry with you, because it was like you were looking down on me, like you thought I didn't want to change. I know I've messed up but I don't want to be like this, it's just how it is at the moment and I do need to get myself out of this mire. I am really in quicksand and I'm sinking so if you ride along on your horse with a lasso, chuck it to me and drag me out.

I love what you all do. I love what you do for the children, and the community. You make a difference in their lives, because there's kids round here ... you try and take them away and give them some understanding about life. So personally I didn't think I could find God, or that I have God in me, but I thought that if I hung around with people that have loads of God about them maybe a little bit would rub off on me and make me feel good.

I know there's a God, I see it in you all, that you people know God. I want to know God. I have found God when I was sober, but I don't find him when I'm drinking, because my god is my bottle. But I know, when I'm sober again, which please God will be very soon, I know I'm going to go and run after him again and chase after him again, say my prayers again and read the Bible. I adore so many of you in the church, I look at you and I think 'I want to be part of it' … I'm slightly envious … I would like to have that in my life, to be part of the church again.

One of the overwhelming messages I get from Tommy is that he wishes people could understand him. It is so easy to look at an alcoholic or a drug addict and judge them, perhaps even now as you read Tommy's words you have thought to yourself, 'Well, if it's that bad, just stop!' But he can't. That is what addiction is. A heroin addict once said to me, 'When I need a fix I can't see anything else except that bag of gear, and I will do anything to get it. If that meant hurting someone or stealing from them – even my family – I would.'

If, like me, you have never been addicted to a substance, it is almost impossible to understand how anyone can feel this way. And maybe this is our first lesson, to acknowledge that unless you have been there you do not fully understand what is going on for an addict. That's not to say that you can be of no use, or that we should all go out and give it a try in order to empathise better, but I regularly make it known when I am with people who have substance misuse issues, that I do not understand but I want to learn what is going on for them and I listen to everything that they say, and over the years I've begun to build up a mental picture of how it all works.

It seems from Tommy's comments that the best thing we can offer as a church is a place to belong, genuine friendship and family. This is what makes him feel like a whole human being again; as I said in the last chapter it is important that we help people to feel the sense of dignity and purpose for which they have been created. Being invited to participate in the normal things of life like having a meal, going to church, watching a movie or just having a game of snooker are all things that remind Tommy that he is more than an alcoholic; he is a human being created by God.

It is interesting to note that he feels let down by the church at times by what he calls 'fair weather friendship'; when he is sober people can't do enough for him, people invite him out and include him socially, we ask for his help with work around the house or the church, but if he is slipping back into old habits he feels left out and excluded from the friendships which he holds so dear, people don't phone and no-one asks for help.

At the time when he needs us most we have a tendency to back away, maybe because we don't know what to say or how to act – perhaps we are fearful that he might upset our civilised social encounters with drunken outbursts; certainly we feel our own sense of disappointment with him, with ourselves and with God. No doubt all of these emotions play their part in his exclusion and in addition Tommy backs away from relationships within the church when he is in his darkest moments. I recognise in myself a subconscious distancing from people when they are using alcohol or drugs, and this must seem a strange response; when they are at their greatest point of need we should be the closest friend.

RECOVERY: A MARATHON NOT A SPRINT

I do believe that God can change lives in an instant and he can set captives free, heal the sick and release the oppressed, but if I am honest the vast majority of the time I have not seen miracles happen before my eyes. Most of the addicts that I know are still addicts – many of them recovering, some clean and dry, some in and out of detox, and others using more heavily than they did when we first met. I don't highlight this to discourage faithful and fervent prayer – in fact I want to encourage such intercession and faith to see the miraculous more often than we have so far – but I want to be honest about the reality of being a church where people with addictions can feel welcome. It is a long hard road and our job is not just to give a slot in our prayer meeting to those afflicted with alcoholism and drug addiction, but to share our lives with such people, through the good times and the bad in the knowledge that unconditional love asks no questions.

In Darkest England we will need to be church communities that accept people with all their baggage, not happy to leave them that way, but happy to travel with them through their darkest moments as well as their great celebrations. You might know that popular old poem called 'Footprints'[4] which describes a person reflecting on their life and noticing two sets of footprints in the sand. In the person's times of struggle the two sets became one, and asking Jesus why this was so he says, 'It was then that I carried you.' A romanticised image maybe, but as we seek to serve those who suffer through addiction we must ensure that when we are asked the question, 'Where were you in my struggle?' we don't answer, 'Well, you were undeserving at that time so we left you to work it out for yourself and came back later.' Matthew 5:45 says that 'He causes his sun to rise on the evil and the good, and sends rain on the righteous and the unrighteous.' It is not our place to judge whether someone is worthy of our help or friendship.

A MIRACLE ON TOXTETH STREET

Karen is about 50 years old and has been using drugs since she was 15. She is from a very normal family, her dad was a military man, she has a brother and two sisters who are all successful in their own field. Karen has been in and out of detox and rehab more than 20 times; the last eight times have been since we have known her. Many times we would take her to detox, check her in and then within 48 hours we would get a phone call to say she had run away so Hannah would go to find her in the middle of the night, stoned at a local haunt, and then they'd go and collect all her things. But things were looking up for Karen and she had gone through a pioneering recovery programme with Turning Point which offered training, routine and some level of employment at the end. We attended her graduation ceremony with the family who were so proud to see her achieve something.

Karen was the life and soul of her cohort, which was made up primarily of drug users and alcoholics but also had a handful of non-drug-using professionals within it who had gone through the training programme for their own benefit or for work purposes. She was the one who made a speech during the graduation and organised flowers for the course leaders – she was in charge.

Quite a few months later, after a long period of sobriety, Karen arrived at our office one morning and she looked ill. All the signs told me immediately that she was using again; she had a dishevelled look, her pupils were reduced to the size of a pinprick, and she was shaking as if it were minus 10 degrees. I invited her in and she explained that she had relapsed but had decided to go 'cold turkey' to sort it out. She was in the middle of unbearable withdrawal, hence the shakes, the sweats and the feeling of terrible cold. She hadn't slept for 48 hours, and having withdrawn from heroin so many times she knew that this torture would go on for four or five days. She was especially bothered about the sleeplessness, saying, 'If only I could sleep through some of this, I could get some energy to face the rest.'

After a long chat which went round in circles a few times, I called Lizzie and Amy who were around the hall that day and we began to pray for Karen, laying hands on her and pleading with God on her behalf for some respite. All the while we could feel her shaking violently, crying and complaining of cold but little by little she calmed and eventually slumped on the desk peacefully. Looking at each other, none of us were sure what we should do so I said quietly to Karen, 'Do you want to lay down?' Then, without hearing an answer, we guided her to a sofa in our hall, laid her on it and covered her with three sleeping bags, and there she stayed for most of the day, sleeping peacefully. We took turns to check on her every half hour and spend some time praying over her throughout the day, and eventually she woke and left. The next day Karen came bounding into our office declaring that she had experienced a miracle. 'I have withdrawn from heroin so many times and I have never slept in the first few days – I don't know anyone who has ever slept in the first few days,' she said. 'That was a miracle.' And I had no reason to disbelieve her.

After this Karen disappeared from our lives, weeks and months went by until eventually three years later, one sunny afternoon Hannah almost literally ran into her in the street. A few hours later Karen was once again sitting eating a meal at our table, it was like a family reunion as we caught up on all the ups and downs since we last talked. After an hour or more I plucked up the courage to ask the question that I had been desperate to ask. 'So ... er ... how was it with the drugs after that day when we prayed for you at the church?' She looked back slightly shocked at the foolishness of my question. 'Well, I've never taken any more drugs since then' she said, as if it were the most normal thing in the world.

THE DIFFICULT MADE IMPOSSIBLE

Recovery, detox and rehab are tough on anyone who has a drug or alcohol dependency and on anyone who finds themselves involved in the process. The cycle of recovery starts by a person acknowledging they have a problem then realising they need help to solve that problem. They then move on to finding and accessing services which can help and getting themselves clean and dry. But the cycle is not complete there – the final stage of the cycle is relapse, where the person slips back into old habits, usually with one small drink or a 'one-off' trip. At this point the exhausting journey begins all over again and everyone involved hopes that this time will be the last time.

I say 'everyone' but actually not everyone is keen for the addict to quit their drug habit, or for the alcoholic to turn teetotal. As a prison inmate you would have wardens and security fencing to stop you breaking out and breathing the fresh air of freedom – as an addict that role is played by those who make their money from peddling intoxicating substances. Our friend Jon was doing really well on his methadone programme, and after years of drug abuse he had managed to stop using heroin altogether and even managed to wean himself off the methadone. This meant for the first time he had made the almost impossible decision to cut himself off from the drug community and cut his ties with most of his associates.

One day there came a knock at the door. It was not his custom to answer the front door unless he was expecting someone so he peered out of the upstairs window to see his dealer on the pavement outside: 'Jon, I know you're in there, let me in,' he shouted. 'I've got some fine gear here for ya,' he said as he held up a small brown packet in full view of the window. Imagine the struggle that this situation induced in the mind of Jon, the long-time heroin addict who has craved the rush of chasing the dragon and longed for the instant gratification of the loaded needle hitting a vein. The temptation was insufferable but Jon remained strong as he continued to observe the dealer's movements and listen to his warm, friendly voice as it promised all that he had missed about using.

Then came the killer blow from a master dealer who knew his customers better than any market trader or car salesman – 'OK mate, no problem – this one's on the house, I'll leave it with you.' The sound of the letterbox rattled round the empty house and the brown package landed on the doormat with a thud. A £10 bag of heroin, the thing that Jon had robbed and lied for during much of his adult life, sitting there on the floor – he had to touch it, he had to move it, he had to remind his fingers what it felt like to hold a full bag again. A few days later Jon was back at the mercy of the dealer, spent out and stoned, but there were no more freebies.

General Booth tells the slightly comical story of Maggie[5] – a terminal, violent alcoholic, known for fighting and sleeping in all manner of unsuitable places, she was befriended by a Salvation Army Captain when she awoke one winter morning with her blood-soaked hair frozen to the floor. Once thawed and released from her unique brand of captivity, Maggie joined the Captain at the barracks where she found the Lord and her sobriety. Her life was transformed for a good deal of time until a 'friend' invited her to drink his health with a glass of lemonade. She took the lemonade without suspecting anything but immediately caught the taste of her old companion, whisky, which had been deliberately slipped into the glass. With the familiar scent in her nostrils and taste on her lips, Maggie headed for the gin palace but, realising what had happened, the brave Army Captain met her there and confronted the barman saying, 'If you dare serve her, I'll break the glass before it reaches her lips. She shall not have any!' And she led Maggie away, back to her new life without the drink.

Desperate times call for desperate measures, and I sometimes wish I'd been more like this Salvation Army Captain, boldly stepping in to prevent vulnerable people doing things they would regret. Perhaps if I had been more like her then Jon would still be alive today, but aged just 33 his life was tragically ended in the summer of 2006 when, after another long period without heroin, he took some bad gear and died alone in a bedsit, just two minutes' walk from our house. When Jon's heartbroken parents came to tell me the news they said that he had been dead for at least two weeks before anyone found him and his body was so badly decomposed they weren't even allowed to see it.

It was a few weeks before the coroner authorised the funeral and as we laid Jon's body to rest there were only his immediate family and a handful of people from the church who attended – none of his drug-using mates, none of the dealers who had kept him locked up for years, not his daughter or her mother; it was a sad, lonely day when all any of us could do was reflect on what we might have done differently.

Addiction is a huge issue in Darkest England and in some way or other the majority of people living in deprived communities are affected by substance misuse and the consequences of it. We must recognise that people who are addicted are real people, who need to be loved and accepted, who deserve to be treated with respect and dignity, who can find freedom and recovery through the miraculous and the ordinary. They are living their lives as captives and the long road to recovery will be full of ups and downs, but the church community must travel the road faithfully through the peaks and the troughs, sticking with our brothers and sisters in success and failure.

The Christian Gospel is a gospel of freedom. Jesus himself claimed that Isaiah 61 is a prophecy concerning his own ministry and one line of that prophecy says, 'He has sent me to proclaim freedom for the prisoners'.[6] Again in John 8:36 he says, 'So if the Son sets you free, you will be free indeed'. These and many other New Testament references to freedom teach us that Jesus' ministry is one of releasing captives, and I believe that applies to those held in the captivity of addiction as much as anybody. Our work must then be equally focused on this difficult and painstaking task. Prepare for disappointment and pray for miracles.

'No amount of reasoning, or earthly or religious considerations, can have any effect upon a man who is so completely under the mastery of this passion that he cannot break away from it, although he sees the most terrible consequences staring him in the face.'[7]

William Booth

References and Notes

1. Church Urban Fund, CUF Poverty Report, August 2006, www.cuf.org.uk/default. asp?id=118 accessed 23/01/07
2. Bancroft, A. et al, 'Summary, Parental drug and alcohol misuse: Resilience and transition among young people', published by the Joseph Rowntree Foundation, 2006
3. In January 2005 Hannah and I moved from the house next door to Tommy to another house about 200 yards away. Tommy helped us move.
4. Fishback Powers, M., *Footprints* (1964).
5. Booth, pp. 160–61.
6. Luke 4:18.
7. Booth, p. 158.

.6 | BUILDING COMMUNITY

The concept of building communities has really been central to everything we've covered so far, but I want to talk more specifically about it in this final chapter. First, we'll look at the need for us to nurture and protect our own relationships within the faith community. Second, we'll explore the benefits of developing networks and partnerships with other people who are doing good things in the areas that we work in. Finally, we will highlight the significance of building up our neighbourhoods, encouraging and engendering pride within them. Each of these aspects is crucial as we become embedded in those hidden places of darkness.

BUILDING OUR FRIENDSHIPS

At this point in the book you could be forgiven for thinking that the prospect of a life in Darkest England sounds pretty grim – the sort of thing that's great to read about but might just be the most miserable thing you can imagine doing yourself. But there is a remarkable paradox at work for those who have made the journey on to some of the estates of Britain to join Eden projects, NEO (New Expressions Of church) communities, and the like. Of course there are periods of frustration and disappointment, even despair sometimes, but the truth is that you don't find these urban missionaries walking around with long faces, depressed at their lot in life or angry with God that he called them to service in the inner city. Quite the contrary is true – for the vast majority of people involved in teams living and serving in poor communities, the experience brings a great sense of joy, fulfilment and even happiness. The places where this is most evident are those where the idea of building community is a high priority; where time, resources and people are dedicated to building a team which has a shared purpose and a commitment to its vision but that feels like a family.

A positive, enjoyable, loving, enduring, committed community or team is an essential part of the mission to Darkest England, and that kind of dynamic does not happen accidentally. For a leader, this may be the thing that takes most of his or her time. This seemingly inward focus may go against our natural instinct to get out in the neighbourhood, doing stuff that connects us with the locals, but investing time building our immediate community of believers will pay back in multiples as we look for long-term, sustainable transformation.

I suppose it has always been nice to have friends – most people enjoy good company and no-one wants to be the person sat on their own at a party or in the school playground – but the societal changes which have engulfed our world in the last century have left us longing for real companions and clinging to genuine friendship like drowning men to driftwood. In post-modern Britain, friends have become an extremely important part of life, especially for the young.

One of the most popular television shows among 'generation X' throughout the late nineties and early millennium years was the American sitcom 'Friends'. Even now, after the cast have long departed the set to enjoy the millions of dollars which the series paid them, the urban legend says that at any time on any day somewhere in the world an episode of 'Friends' is showing. 'Friends' is a long-running comedy account of the lives of six young adults who share every aspect of their lives.

From time to time references are made to other family members and there are occasional cameo appearances introducing new characters (usually played by A-list celebrities looking to gain even greater credibility by appearing on this show), but ultimately life always returns to the six friends. The episodes journey through ups and downs, relationships on and relationships off, jobs come and go, and the friends fall out and fall back in again, but there is a depth of relationship which holds these six people together. They are in fact a pseudo-family; a tight unit defined by unconditional love and acceptance that seem unbreakable even in the most desperate times.

Why would a series built on such foundations be so incomparably popular in these days? Undoubtedly it has much to do with the genius of the script writers and an unnaturally beautiful cast. But there is an even greater draw for many in our society, where family life has been eroded either through relationship failure among parents, rebellion of children or simply geographical distance, which separates far more of us from our nearest and dearest than was true a hundred years ago.

We crave the intimacy that comes from family life and the stability that it gives us through dependable relationships, and when that has been lost for so many, then good strong friendships become a prized asset, something to be sought after and cherished when found. What we see when we watch 'Friends' is something that looks and feels a bit like family but isn't, and seems more attainable to us than a properly functioning, real family. It looks and feels a bit like reality, but it isn't.

The family was once the foundation of working-class communities. It would not be unusual to find three or four units of the same family living on the same street, and sometimes generation after generation would grow up in the same house. Nowadays these supportive, close-knit family networks are less common; many people have become estranged from their relatives and cut their path in life alone. Shelly is one such example. When she was 16, her mum got a new boyfriend who didn't want her around so her mum told her, 'You're a pretty girl, you'll get on in life', and sent her out on her own.

The first person who could offer her anything that felt remotely like family in terms of love, comfort and lodgings was a pimp and drug dealer who took her in and led her into a life of prostitution and narcotics. When I see her now in her mid-20s, looking at least 40, I wonder how different life might have been if at her point of need she had made her way to a church and that church was able to become the community which she called home.

One of the great things about being part of a church community is that it offers us the family that so many of us crave, and that is how it should be. I once heard someone say that if you go to a church and there are no unusual people there then something is wrong; if there are no social misfits, no weirdoes, no people with body odour, no people who have poor social skills ... then the question is 'why not?' What is it about this church that repels people who don't fit in? The church should be the one place where everyone can feel they belong.

Jesus said in John 13:34–35: 'A new command I give you: Love one another. As I have loved you, so you must love one another. By this all men will know that you are my disciples, if you love one another.'

This is obviously incredibly important to Jesus, who doesn't generally display a great deal of passion for rules and traditions throughout the Gospels, but here creates a new commandment, repeated in John 15:12. Love in the Christian community is commanded by Jesus himself, who knew just what an amazing witness that love would be to a world which has such a poor understanding of what love is.

One of the key aspects of our community programme at the Eden Project in Openshaw is the Family Support Project, which is funded by SureStart and supports families with children of all ages, but especially those with kids under 5 years old. Part of our work with those families is done through Adult and Toddler sessions. We started with one group, then two, then three, then we added a baby group and a baby church. Each time we add a session it fills up, with more mums, dads, grandparents and kids coming in to participate in the interactive sessions. This may seem unspectacular, but in our area it is a phenomenon.

The truth is that all the other toddler groups in our neighborhood find it difficult to get anyone to attend, struggling on at huge cost to the local council with one or two families attending. So stark is the contrast between our group and the other groups that our Family Support Worker, Nicci, was recently asked at a SureStart meeting, 'What is it about your group that makes it work?' The answer is that we are building community, not just running sessions. We care about the people who come in; they get looked after, they get visited, we become friends with them, and people crave that kind of experience so they come – and they stay.

Whether we are part of a team which moves from other places to work in an area, or a local person who is looking for the support of a church, the key element will be what kind of 'family' we find when we connect with the church. Churches often pride themselves on being 'friendly'. What that often means is that you get a firm handshake at the door and a cup of tea afterwards if you're lucky. But I'm not sure that today's world is interested in 'friendly'.

Have you ever been to one of those shops that sell film merchandise for kids? They're usually American and someone greets you at the door as you walk in with a 'Hi there', and as you leave they say 'Have a nice day'. How does their friendliness make you feel? Maybe I am cynical but it makes me want to go away and come back after I've worked out how to make myself invisible so that, just once, I could walk into the shop without hearing the insincere 'friendly' greeting which they bleat out to every customer. I can get 'friendliness' in a dozen such places but it just puts me off.

When people come to church what they want to discover is not friendliness but friends, people who are genuinely interested and loving, people who want to hang out and have coffee, help with the kids or go to the park. Christians in 'friendly' churches are often very good at inviting people to more church activities but not so good at sharing their lives with those who they come into contact with. Building community will require that we make space in our busy lives to be friends, not just friendly – that might mean sacrificing some of our church programmes, but if it means we have space in our lives to connect properly with the people around us then it will be a sacrifice worth making.

General Booth recognised the need for building community throughout his book as he proposed his different 'colonies': the city colony, the farm colony and the overseas colony. He envisaged that these three types of community would, like the rungs of a ladder, be steps out of poverty. 'I have now sketched out briefly the leading features of the threefold Scheme by which I think a way can be opened out of "Darkest England"'.[1] 'The Scheme I have to offer consists in the formation of these people into self helping and self sustaining communities, each being a kind of co-operative society, or patriarchal family.'[2]

As much as Booth saw his vision as benefiting individuals, he knew that an important part of their salvation would be discovered through building positive communities. His desire to create patriarchal families demonstrates his understanding that it is not possible to communicate a gospel of love from any other context than a community of love. If our church families are places devoid of meaningful relationships, then any claims that we may make to knowing a God of love will surely be meaningless until people can see that love evidenced among the faithful.

Once again, for Booth the communities were initiated in order to help people find their way out of Darkest England and on to a better life; I believe that the call for us now is to go right back into the heart of our toughest neighbourhoods and establish vibrant, loving communities right there in the midst of all the brokenness and disappointment.

Our God himself exists in community: Father, Son and Holy Spirit. Jesus commanded us to love our neighbors as ourselves, and when we live by his example and according to his instruction then our light will shine in the darkness.

BUILDING OUR NETWORKS

When you arrive in Darkest England you are likely to discover that you and your team are not the first or only people who are trying to do positive things there. One of the first people I met in Openshaw was Bob, a taxi driver who often parked his cab at the back of our building, and one day I got chatting to him. He was interested to know what all the activity was in and around the building and when I explained what we were doing he was fascinated because he had teenaged children, and along with some other parents who were concerned about their kids, they had just started a youth club in the local school. We worked with Bob over the years and he is now one of the key players in the youth and community sector for East Manchester, involved in lots of work and responsible for the distribution of significant amounts of money to projects like ours. Our relationship with Bob has been an encouragement to us and to him; it has enhanced all our work and made it better, it has given us access to funding streams which we otherwise may not have know about and it helps us to have a 'joined-up' approach to work in Openshaw.

One of our first tasks when we arrived in Openshaw was to contact all the agencies and churches who were working in our area at the time. We arranged meetings with representatives from all those groups, and the meetings all had the same format: we would start the meeting by very briefly explaining who we are and asking, 'Are there gaps in youth provision for this area that we could try to fill, and are there any other ways that we can serve your project?' We thought this a better approach than bombarding people with all our ideas and dreams for our project and we genuinely did want to serve the community in whatever way we could. In every case we got a warm reception, lukewarm in some cases but warm nevertheless – except for one: a local church leader whose response to our initial phone call was to say, 'I know who you are, I don't agree with what you're doing and I won't work with you'. We were totally thrown by this response but our hunch was that we should keep trying to build community with him and little by little he warmed to us, talked to us and even worked with us on a few things. Some of our guys went down regularly to help with his Sunday afternoon meeting, then one Sunday morning about three years after this initial telephone conversation he walked into our church just as our morning meeting ended, wanting to talk to me. In a quiet corner, as our post-church chaos and noise whirred around us, he said to me, 'I have some young people in my church and I am not sure I have what they need but I think you do, so could I send them there?' Of course we said yes to the young people, but more importantly we said yes to partnership with his church, we said yes to community, and we said yes to family. How ironic that out of all the dozens of people we met from the council, the youth service, social services, regeneration partners and voluntary sector organisations, the most sceptical person with the biggest objection to our presence was a brother from another church. On reflection, I should not really have been surprised by that – in my experience the church often shies away from working in partnership with others, whether they be secular agencies or other churches, and I know that in my years as a church youth worker I was quite reluctant to work with others.

Perhaps we feel threatened or insecure, worried that our work isn't up to standard. Maybe we are worried that if we join with another organisation our identity will be lost or our 'cutting edge' will be blunted. It is likely that neither of these are true; contrary to what we often think of ourselves the church is widely recognised to make an important contribution to communities by doing good quality, sustainable work which is well respected across the sectors. In my experience of partnership work it is widely understood that whenever organisations work together there will be issues to iron out regarding preservation of identity, so those are relatively easy discussions to have as long as we know who we are and what we are trying to achieve. If we remain isolated, untouchable islands of activity, our work will be limited to the parameters of our own expertise, our growth will be stunted to the size of our own budgets and our credibility and reputation will stretch no further than our own backyard.

A friend spoke to me recently about a project her church is on the verge of starting. The project looked fantastic, and the church had been dreaming this up for nearly two years. It involved working with struggling families, providing parenting classes, supporting the parents through numeracy and literacy courses and mentoring them into employment. The whole thing was really well thought out and professionally presented in a colour booklet. When I asked her where the families would be referred from she looked quite blank, so I simplified the question: 'Where will the families come from? Are they people that you already know or are they being referred to you from another organisation?' There was a pause. 'Well, we don't really know any families who would need this but we know there is a big need in our area.' I tried another question: 'What other groups are working with these type of families in your community?' I could see a pattern emerging: 'I'm not really sure.' The church had put lots of time and energy into planning what has potential to be a hugely effective and successful project, but they had not yet sought any connection with other people providing or receiving similar services in their community. This approach is fraught with problems. We need to build our networks, and a good place to start is to go to the people that know your community and its services best and say 'We'd like to do something, how can we help to make our neighborhood better?'

Booth had a greater appreciation for the value of networks than many evangelical activists that went before and many who have come after him. He claims that the task of reforming the Social System is beyond any one of us and even beyond 'all of us put together'.[3] It was obvious to Booth that the challenges faced by the underclasses then were too many and varied for one person or one organisation to attempt to meet all the needs. In spite of his incredible passion and vision he was aware of his own inadequacy for the task, saying, 'I am ready to sit at the feet of any who will show me any good'.[4]

This is a statement which demonstrates a vulnerability and willingness to learn from others, a trait which is perhaps all too rare in the church today. He would not be surprised that after a hundred years we have not yet solved the problem of urban poverty, and he would be shocked if The Salvation Army were ever to stop trying.

BUILDING OUR COMMUNITIES

The Home Office maintain an ongoing piece of research called The Indices of Deprivation.[5] This inverted league table compares all the 32,482 thousand wards across the UK on the basis of their socioeconomic status. Each community is judged on issues such as crime, health, the value of property, unemployment and household income.

Each year one community wins the coveted prize of being crowned 'worst place to live in Britain'; the national papers love to run these stories, which are inevitably illustrated by pictures of burnt-out cars, boarded-up houses or piles of rubbish in alleyways. And as the nation looks on and turns up a collective nose at the squalid conditions that 'some people' live in, so the reputation of the places who came in the top few percent of deprived communities is further diminished, the self-esteem of the people who live in those places is dealt another blow, and the communities that are fighting for survival are submerged once more.

The indices of deprivation should become our tool for working out where our light is going to shine next. Booth once said, 'Go for souls and go for the worst', and I believe that if he was reading the concluding chapter of this book he would be saying, 'Go for communities and go for the worst'. As we consider now our response to twenty-first-century Darkest England, let's not just look for neighbourhoods slightly less well off than our own. Our eyes should be set on the top 5 per cent of most deprived communities in Britain and that is where we should go to build those communities and begin to live out our transformational mandate.

For many in Darkest England, the decades of decline have taken their toll. The years of longing for the day when their beloved neighbourhood would be recognised for something other than deprivation have left them without a hope for themselves, for their children or for their children's children. We can change that, and in fact we must change that.

Building community means being ambassadors of hope who believe things can be better. Building a community means learning to love it 'warts and all'; it means noticing the good things and pointing them out to people who have forgotten how to notice; it means laughing at some of the silliness that happens on the streets knowing that it is harmless.

Building a community means speaking well of it to everyone who will listen, reflecting on its failures honestly but with a positive attitude and vocabulary. It means investing sacrificially in it, joining the residents' association, coaching the local kids' football team, singing carols at Christmas, creating community events and being an activist.

It means long-term commitments that help to stabilise the often fluid population. And it means having a dream of what this place can be with a little encouragement, some positive action and a greater awareness of the Kingdom of God which is all around. We need to be the kind of people who engender pride and passion in the places we live in, helping people to see that there are diamonds in the dust and that the future can be better than the present.

It is easy to fall into the trap of advertising all the bad aspects of our communities. I know, because I have done it. Sometimes I know that when I've been invited to speak, or when we have produced our newsletters, I have majored too much on the negatives of Openshaw through the stories that I tell and the articles that I write. I have noticed that there is a kind of macabre interest in the dark side of a ministry like ours. I was at a conference recently and was introduced to a guest speaker from another country whose eyes lit up when he realised that I was involved in the Eden project. He shook my hand fiercely and said, 'Gary, wow, I heard someone got killed doing mission in Openshaw!' When I told him that this was news to me, he seemed overcome with disappointment and my reputation returned to that of a mortal man again.

I have learned to be more balanced, and I hope that this book itself is balanced. I want to be honest about the realities of life in dark communities and ministry among the urban poor, but I also want to speak positively about it at every opportunity. I honestly believe that living out our Christian faith in tough communities can be the most joy-filled, fulfilling thing that any of us might do with the years we have on this earth. I love living in our community; I love the people there, they are my friends, and in many cases they deserve better than they get so I want to try to get a better deal for them in life and for eternity.

REBUILDING THE CITY

Several years ago, as we spent a weekend praying together in our church, there was a sense amongst us that we were being led to explore a particular passage of scripture. Isaiah 62 is a prophecy from 500 BC concerning the renewal of the city of Jerusalem as the great nation of Israel returned there after years in exile, and we have claimed its regenerative sentiments for the terraced streets of Openshaw. Some may ask what relevance this passage can possibly have for a twenty-first-century church in Manchester, but these promises embody the redemptive purpose of God for all manner of contexts and communities.

The book of Isaiah has several themes running through it, one of which is to do with 'former things' and 'later things' – this is evident in chapter 62, which opens:

For Zion's sake I will not keep silent,
for Jerusalem's sake I will not remain quiet,
till her righteousness shines out like the dawn,
her salvation like a blazing torch. (v. 1)

This chapter promises that Jerusalem will no longer be called deserted or desolate but instead will be called Hephzibah, which means 'my delight is in her', and Beulah, which means 'married'. The significance of these names is that they bestow beauty and dignity on the city.

The idea of a city or community being married may seem strange, but its meaning is that whereas a woman who is widowed or divorced will not bear any children, a woman who is married can bear children and have many descendants. When a community is described by God as Beulah or 'married', He means that it will bear fruit and that many good things can come from it.

This illustrates that the former things have gone, 'You will build a house, but not live in it' (Deut 28:30), 'You will plant a vineyard but will not drink its wine' (Amos 5:11), but in the new order, in the latter days, things will be different. 'But those who harvest it will eat it and praise the LORD, and those who gather the grapes will drink it in the courts of my sanctuary' (Is 62:9). The promise is one of a great harvest from our land, and in Openshaw we are living in that promise, expecting there to be great salvation, new inhabitants, a restored righteousness and great spiritual giants, growing up in our midst as God himself rejoices over Openshaw.

Building community happens in all kinds of ways. Sometimes it happens unexpectedly when we see someone in the street or the launderette, and we must be aware of every opportunity, never avoiding those impromptu conversations, eye contact or a cheerful 'good morning'. However, we should not leave this to chance; spending time and resources on intentional relationship building is essential, and our schedules and diaries should have adequate space for us to be friends. As we do this, morale will consequentially improve in the places that we live and we can go about the business of shouting about the good things in our neighborhood, noticing the positives and pointing out the Kingdom of God which is all around.

'There is no sanctimonious long face in the Army. We are happy, and we wish others to share our joy. We know by our own experience that life is a very different thing when we have found the peace of God, and are working together with Him for the Salvation of the world.'[7]

William Booth

References and Notes

1. Booth, p. 137.
2. Booth, p. 82.
3. Booth, p. 36.
4. Booth, p. 71.
5. You can view these on www.communities.gov.uk/index.asp?id=1128439.
6. Eden Openshaw covers three Super Output Areas that are listed as numbers 11, 12 and 206 out of 32,482.
7. Booth, p. 100.

POSTSCRIPT – HIDDEN TRACKS

The twenty-first-century church has a challenge at its doorstep, a challenge that causes us to consider the dark reality of life for the urban poor who live largely out of the sight and the minds of the middle and upper classes. We must once again allow our hearts to be stirred by the plight of those living in desperate poverty across the UK and indeed the world. We must search the scriptures again and rediscover just how concerned God is for those living in the margins and how significant our response to them is.

As a reader of this book I want to thank you for sticking with it to the end. There have probably been points at which it would have been easier to put the book down or send it to the charity shop. I hope it has been more than interesting – I hope that it has challenged you and caused you to question your own response to Darkest England and those who live there. What will you do now? In approximately five minutes you will have the deeply satisfying feeling of finishing a book and returning it to the shelf, but if all the reading has been worth anything, it must provoke a response. As the author of this book, I have lived with the writing side of it for about six months and I know its contents from cover to cover, but what happens after the final page (in my life and in yours) are as yet unknown – they are the hidden tracks which are yet to be discovered. My prayer is that the end of my book marks the beginning of your own personal adventure into Darkest England, and that we all go on to write the next part of the story together.

Towards the end of *In Darkest England and The Way Out*, General Booth makes some summarising comments which bear a great deal of relevance to the proposals which I have made. He makes it clear that the work he has outlined in his book is the most important work of The Salvation Army, that the work on behalf of the poor should not be eclipsed by any other aspect of service or activity which the Army engages in. This is a challenge not just to members of the Army, but to all of us who call ourselves followers of Jesus. How easy it is to fill our lives with other things

– meetings, discussions, social events and conferences – but forget the main responsibilities that we have been entrusted with. He acknowledges that the whole scheme will 'strain resources to the utmost'; many more recruits are needed to join the workforce that will turn his great dream into a reality. My involvement with the wider Eden project and with the NEO communities has shown me that there is never any shortage of need in these communities, but the hardest things to find are people – good people, especially gifted leaders and finances to run the initiatives with, and most noticeably in the early stages. Perhaps you are able to join a team or support financially – if you are in a wealthy church you could support a local project, maybe if you're in a big church you could send a team to live and minister on a nearby housing estate. Booth says we shouldn't worry that we can't do everything, there is an important role for everyone to play in the redemption of Darkest England. Urban mission teams don't need eight loud extroverts (one of those is usually more than enough . . .), dynamic preachers or athletic sportsmen, they need a mixture of personality types, skills and gifts, and young or old you could be more significant than your imagination will dare to tell you.

Doing nothing is not an option. When the Apostle Paul went to Jerusalem with Barnabas and Titus (Gal 2), he found favour with Peter, James and John, who were reputed to be the pillars of the church. It was decided that Paul and Barnabas would preach the Gospel to the Gentiles while the others would continue to minister to the Jews. In verse 10 Paul recalls, 'All they asked was that we should continue to remember the poor.' Of all the instructions that could have been given at this crucial point in church history, they chose this. If it had been me I would probably have wanted to ensure that their theology was correct, or that their outreach strategies were properly administrated, but they chose this one instruction because it strikes at the core of everything that we do and everything that we are as the church of Jesus Christ. Ignoring or disassociating ourselves from the submerged masses of our world is not an option for me or for you. Where will the hidden tracks of your life lead now? I hope that in some way or other they will lead you to those that are waiting for you in Darkest England.

I will leave the last words to Booth, for whom my admiration has grown so much throughout this journey:

'The plan has now been published to the world; it is for you to say whether it will remain barren, or whether it is to bear fruit in unnumbered blessings to all the children of men.'
William Booth

GOING FURTHER

If reading *Darkest England* has left you itching to get involved then below you can find details of just two of the many organisations who are building church in areas of urban deprivation.

SALVATION ARMY NEO PROJECTS

NEO creates new expressions of church that see the broken repaired, the hurting healed and the desperate enjoying hope. It recruits teams to move into some of the poorest neighbourhoods in the UK and Republic of Ireland to build community and provide experiences that transform.

http://web.salvationarmy.org.uk/alove/neo_homepage.asp

MESSAGE TRUST EDEN PROJECTS

Eden is an award-winning and influential approach to urban youth-work and community transformation. The really unique thing about Eden is the way the teams choose to live in the most difficult areas, sharing the problems of those growing up there, and ministering to their needs. We believe it's truly Jesus-style ministry. Eden is part of a family of pioneering youth ministries operated by The Message Trust. The Message is passionate about young people, believing that whatever their circumstances, they shouldn't be excluded from an opportunity to hear about the amazing love of God.

http://www.message.org.uk

Notes